MAKING GOVE|

VOLU

MW00577582

The Promises and Pitfalls of Performance-Informed Management

Katherine Barrett and Richard Greene

Foreword by Peter Harkness

ROWMAN & LITTLEFIELD
Lanham ▪ Boulder ▪ New York ▪ London

Executive Editor: Traci Crowell
Assistant Editor: Deni Remsberg
Higher Education Channel Manager: Jonathan Raeder

Credits and acknowledgments for material borrowed from other sources, and reproduced with permission, appear on the appropriate page within the text.

Published by Rowman & Littlefield
An imprint of The Rowman & Littlefield Publishing Group, Inc.
4501 Forbes Boulevard, Suite 200, Lanham, Maryland 20706
www.rowman.com

6 Tinworth Street, London SE11 5AL, United Kingdom

British Library Cataloguing in Publication Information Available

Library of Congress Cataloging-in-Publication Data
Names: Barrett, Katherine, 1954- author. | Greene, Richard, 1955- author.
Title: Making government work: the promises and pitfalls of performance-informed management / Katherine Barrett, Richard Greene.
Description: Lanham, Maryland: Rowman & Littlefield, 2020. | Includes bibliographical references and index.
Identifiers: LCCN 2019046456 | ISBN 9781538125670 (cloth) | ISBN 9781538125687 (paperback) | ISBN 9781538125694 (epub)
Subjects: LCSH: Government accountability—United States. | Public administration—United States—Evaluation. | Administrative agencies—United States—Management. | Government productivity—United States. | Organizational effectiveness—United States.
Classification: LCC JK421 .B275 2020 | DDC 352.6/6—dc23
LC record available at https://lccn.loc.gov/2019046456

♾️™ The paper used in this publication meets the minimum requirements of American National Standard for Information Sciences—Permanence of Paper for Printed Library Materials, ANSI/NISO Z39.48–1992.

This book is dedicated to Nancy Barrett, with our love and thanks for her immeasurable quest to bring happiness to the world.

Contents

■ ■ ■

viii ■ Contents

viii ■ Contents

Resources	138
Glossary	142
Notes	147
Index	157

Acknowledgments

■ ■ ■

ABOUT THREE DECADES AGO, when we first started exploring the field of performance management (although at the time we were calling it "managing for results"), a great many people in the public sector and in the press were minimally conscious of the phenomenon. After writing a long feature about it, long before we were associated with *Governing* magazine, one of our editors went on a radio show and described our work as being about pay for performance. That was quite an embarrassment.

But in all the years that have passed, we've been increasingly intrigued by performance management efforts. As things stand, we fall somewhere in between describing ourselves as skeptics and zealots.

We are not academics, and although we have participated in academic exercises, we're journalists at heart. As a result, we've had the pleasure of interviewing a seemingly endless list of practitioners, elected officials, academics, organization leaders, and so on. This approach, we always felt, benefited us tremendously by giving us the opportunity to go beyond simple commentary as you'd find in survey forms, and to ask follow-up questions, and follow-up questions to the follow-up questions.

We'd like to take this opportunity to give rich thanks to a number of the men and women who educated us about performance management. In some cases, they were interviewed specifically for this book, in an effort to make it as timely as possible. In others, they have been our mentors for a number of years, helping us find our way to the on-ramp to the performance measurement highway. We apologize if we've missed any names. But among those who we view as particularly important supporters of our work and generous suppliers of context and information from the early stages on are Terrell Blodget, Jonathan Bruel, Jay Fountain, Deborah Kerr, Mark Funkhouser, Harry Hatry, John Kamensky, Shelley Metzenbaum, Scott Pattison, and Marv Weidner.

We would be remiss to leave out the men and women of the Pew Charitable Trusts and *Governing* magazine, who made the Government Performance Project (GPP) possible. They include Michele Mariani Vaughn, whom we jokingly called our "partner in crime," as she, herself, did excessive amounts of work to keep us from collapsing under the weight of the project's inhuman workload. Others at the magazine always had our backs during the GPP years: Alan Ehrenhalt, Peter Harkness, Elder Witt, and Zach Patton, who acted as a reporter for us in the GPP and was executive editor at *Governing* magazine, until it ceased publication after the September 2019 issue. Additionally, Susan Urahn at Pew was instrumental in providing moral and internal support at the Pew Charitable Trusts.

We want to give a special mention to a couple of men who weren't with us at the very beginning of this journey but have been unstintingly available to us in this work: Don Kettl and Philip Joyce.

And now comes the long list of men and women whom we consulted, interviewed, and checked information with. Some of them were instrumental along the way before we wrote word one, page one of this book; others joined in as we did the research directly intended for it, and still others helped us to procure images or to find documents. We were tempted to describe each individual's contribution (to separate the people who spent hours on the phone with us from others who pointed us to a document). But that would have led to a seemingly endless list of acknowledgments, and we chose, instead, to devote that space to chapters in the book itself.

We thank:

Joel Alter, David Ammons, Larisa Benson, Barbara Cohn Berman, Randall Bauer, Gary Blackmer, Ralph Blumenthal, Melissa Bridges,

Inger Brinck, John Cape, Jim Chrisinger, Paul Decker, Amy Donahue, Sara Dube, Sam Edelstein, Amy Edwards, Sharon Erickson, Alexandra Fercak, Adria Finch, Myron Frans, Susan Fritzlen, Benjamin Greene, Sandra Greene, Al Gore, Lori Grange, Frank Fairbanks, Myron Frans, David Gottesman, Jed Herrmann, John Hicks, Marc Holzer, Maia Jachimowicz, Michael Jacobson;

Hollie Jensen, Crista Johnson, Neal Johnson, Anne Jordan, Chris Kelly, Chelsea Lei, Penelope Lemov, Jim Lewis, Gary Locke, Megan Macvie, Zachary Markovits, Curt Marshall, Kelly Martinelli, Melissa Maynard, Nick Mastronadi, Heidi McGregor, Chris Mihm, Rakesh Mohan, Don Moynihan, Melissa Schigoda, Ken Miller, Jerry Newfarmer, Kimberly Olivares;

Cory Poris Plasch, Brooks Rainwater, Robin Rosenberg, Charles Sallee, Torey Salloway, Melissa Schigoda, Sherry Schoonover, Susan Sieg, Steven Rathgeb Smith, David Smith, Kathryn Stack, Brent Stockwell, Paul Taylor, Leah Tivoli, Susan Sieg Tompkins, Dick Tracy, Jeffrey Tryens, John Turcotte, Diana Urban, Ed Van Eenoo, Gary VanLandingham, James Wagner, Jonathan Walters, Melissa Wavelet, Darcy White, Kathryn Vesey White, Gaye Williams, Kathryn Newcomer, Juan Urbano, Katherine Willoughby, Quentin Wilson, Will Wilson, Oliver Wise, J.B. Wogan, and Lyle Wray.

We would also like to thank the reviewers of this text: Donald F. Kettl (University of Texas at Austin), Andrew Kleine, Lyle D. Wray (Metro State University), Deborah L. Kerr (Texas A&M University), and Alexandra Fercak.

Two final thank yous: one to our long-(long!)-time agent Stuart Krichevsky and the other to the people at our publisher Rowman & Littlefield, who have been cheerleaders, supporters, implementers, and all-around good folks: Traci Crowell and Deni Remsberg.

Preface

■ ■ ■

ALTHOUGH SOME SOURCES cite a larger number, there are at least a dozen words for snow used by the Inuit people of Alaska and northern Canada.

That may be a cliché, but it is clear that the subject of this book—performance management—is a lot like that. Those two words represent a broad range of approaches and practices aimed at managing effectively, budgeting wisely, prioritizing programs, and so on.

As performance management has evolved, it has encompassed many different tools and approaches including measurement, data analysis, evidence-based management, process improvement, research, and evaluation. In the past, many of the efforts to improve performance in government have been fragmented, separated into silos, and labeled with a variety of different names including performance-based budgeting, performance-informed management, managing for results, and so on.

Whatever you call it, performance management is essential to well-run governments—at all levels from special districts to cities, counties, states, and the federal government. Unlike private sector firms, which can claim victory when profits go up, things are much trickier for government. Enter performance management as a means for gauging degrees of success and failure in governmental work, and then making decisions based on that understanding.

This book is loaded with dozens of stories related to us by practitioners—what's working, what's not. The benefits are ample and so are the challenges. This book describes both, along with practical steps taken by practitioners to make government work better.

Many books that tackle various aspects of public administration, we have noted, tend to rely on examples that can be years, even decades, old. For some government management disciplines this may be useful and even appropriate. But performance management has been in a state of evolution for decades now, and so we have endeavored to capture the state of the world as it is today.

As you read on, you will discover that while we strive to meet the documentation standards of carefully vetted academic papers, the approach we take is journalistic. Over the last year we've talked to scores of state and local officials, as well as academics and other national experts, to find out how performance management tools and approaches have changed, and what is coming in the near-term future. This was importantly supplemented by digging deeply into documents to find yet more examples from states and localities and to verify the accuracy of the major points made by our interviewees. We even went through storage closets full of the files we've accumulated on this topic over decades.

Our background in this field goes back to 1990, when we first began evaluating the status of performance management in all fifty states as well as the largest cities and counties. We were, in those early years, pioneers in covering this field outside of academic papers. We proudly quote Peter Harkness, founder of *Governing* magazine, as writing about twenty years ago that we were "by far the most experienced journalists in the country covering public performance." We would like to believe that is still the case.

There have always been, and continue to be, naysayers about the value of measuring results or the quantity of work done (outcomes and outputs, in the jargon of the field). About twenty-five years ago, the budget director of one New England state told us that, as far as he was concerned, using measurements to help improve policy was a notion that was "dying off one zealot at a time." We disagreed, publicly, in a meeting people were talking about for years.

We believe that much naysaying has been nurtured by a large body of writing, including other books that preceded this one, that set performance management forth as a panacea. When that turns out not to be the case, people lose faith, public servants resist, and sought-after accomplishments can be stymied.

It is our hope that by providing both challenges and conquests of performance management in this book, we can provide readers with the kind of balanced information that informs both academics and practitioners and can move the field forward.

About the Authors

■ ■ ■

OVER THE COURSE of nearly thirty years, Katherine Barrett and Richard Greene, principals of Barrett and Greene, Inc., have done much-praised analysis, research, and writing about state and local governments, with a concentration on performance management. They were founders of the Government Performance Project, funded by the Pew Charitable Trusts, and for twenty years wrote columns for *Governing* magazine, often about performance-related issues. Following the shutdown of *Governing* magazine, they are continuing to write about these topics for Route Fifty. They worked with the Governmental Accounting Standards Board on its Service Efforts and Accomplishments initiative. Greene is currently chair of the Center for Accountability and Performance at the American Society for Public Administration (ASPA).

Foreword

■ ■ ■

OVER MY ENTIRE CAREER I've been surrounded by journalists dedicated to covering government, public policy, and politics at every level. They have immersed themselves in the intricacies of legislative provisions, regulations, and back-room deal-making. But for various reasons there is one key area that did not attract their interest—how governments manage themselves. Even though it undoubtedly is critical to success in the public sector, management still is seen as inherently boring, too in-the-weeds for consumers of news and for journalists themselves. Just leave that to the bureaucrats and academics.

Enter Katherine Barrett and Richard Greene, the authors of *Making Government Work: The Promises and Pitfalls of Performance-Informed Management*. Over three decades, Katherine and Richard (or B&G, as they have become known to their many admirers) have covered in detail every facet of how state and local governments manage themselves, their millions of employees, their myriad systems for handling finances, collecting taxes, educating children, dispensing healthcare, purchasing goods and services, maintaining infrastructure, and on and on.

The single area to which they've likely made the most significant contributions, both as writers and as consultants to a range of public sector—oriented organizations, is performance management. This book is not just the culmination of decades of experience in the field but is also journalistically based, with the most recent-possible examples and case studies—unlike many other books that rely on information that's ten or twenty years old.

Years ago I described B&G as "by far the most experienced journalists in the country covering public performance." If anything, that is truer today than it was back then. Fortunately, they emerged at the right time. *Governing* magazine was launched more than three decades ago by the Congressional Quarterly news service (well known as CQ), which had prospered by focusing solely on the U.S. Congress in laborious detail. But *Governing* was radically different.

It would cover all subgovernments: states, cities, counties, regions, even port authorities, as well as their relations with the feds. How did these disparate governments at all levels improve the efficiency and effectiveness of their programs, departments, and agencies? What worked and what didn't? For B&G it was a perfect fit; they not only understood it but could explain it.

One significant contribution B&G made to improving public management generally, and performance management in particular, involved an ambitious program funded by the Pew Charitable Trusts and published in *Governing* known as the Government Performance Project. It was an unusual effort teaming journalists with academics to evaluate the performance of all fifty states and many of the nation's largest cities and counties.

The GPP was published for eleven straight years and won two nominations for the National Magazine Award—no small feat when the competition included the *New Yorker* and the *Atlantic*. Katherine and Richard not only conducted countless interviews across the country for the project, they also analyzed the interview findings as well as those provided by the academics, and served as the principal authors of the final reports.

In the ensuing years, Barrett and Greene continued delving into the topic and disseminating their knowledge through dozens of speeches from coast to coast and a variety of print and online media.

Greene (in one of the rare instances when either member of the team operates separately from the other) has served for a couple of years as the chair of the Center on Accountability and Performance at ASPA.

They have just joined the well-respected Route Fifty, where they will continue to produce regular columns, including those about performance management.

Upon reading the book I was immediately struck by their ability to thoroughly cover the most important elements of performance management in a way that is thoroughly documented and still thoroughly readable—even entertaining.

They drew upon scores of interviews with many of the most knowledgeable men and women in this country who specialize in the performance management realm. Academics and practitioners can both benefit from this work. I'm a journalist and editor. And I did.

Peter Harkness
Founder of *Governing* magazine

1
Overview

■ ■ ■

ALMOST THIRTY YEARS AGO, we began work on an evaluation of
the management capacity of the states for a now-defunct magazine
called *Financial World*. Among the categories we wanted to explore
were budgeting, human resources, and infrastructure.

But after conversations with dozens of public administration
experts, we discovered that we'd be shortchanging our readers by
ignoring performance management.

Our work was warmly received. This was particularly true as it
was the only source available to give academics, public sector leaders,
and other interested parties a sense of the wide range of practices
available in each one of the fifty states.

That project provided the roots for the Government Performance
Project (GPP), funded by the Pew Charitable Trusts and appearing
in *Governing* magazine. That effort, which involved a squadron of
academics as well as a team of journalists, kept tabs on positive and
negative trends in the states for a dozen years. It ended almost ten
years ago, but we have continued to write and research extensively
about the use of a variety of data to help make difficult decisions at
the state and local levels.

In the early years of our own work, we focused very closely
on performance measurement—how governments chose what they
wanted to accomplish, both in the short and long terms; established

goals and targets; and how they then measured the trend lines for actual results as well as changes in the level of work and money dedicated to making improvement.

But providing good accurate information to managers, decision makers, and citizens only provides a partially completed puzzle. Performance management encompasses many different tools that have appeared, morphed, diminished, disappeared, reappeared, grown, and matured over time.

Performance management efforts, whether they involve tracking and analyzing data, benchmarking against other government entities, streamlining management through process improvement, or utilizing evaluations that provide evidence of past program success, have been structured in countless ways over time. They are often under-resourced, resisted by busy departments, and are vulnerable to shifts in political leadership.

In chapter 7 of this book, we'll be elaborating on a series of specific pitfalls that may lie in the path of useful performance management. But, to kick things off, following are some general issues with which state and local governments must grapple in order to hope for successful excursions into this territory.

© iStock/Getty Images Plus/DigitalVision Vectors

2
Challenges

■ ■ ■

NOWADAYS, LEADERS IN CITIES, counties, states, and the federal government will generally say that they are engaged in performance management and that they measure what they do. But upon closer questioning, it evolves that the performance rhetoric is often loftier than what is happening in actual practice.

Take, for example, dashboards and other efforts to display performance information to enterprise-wide managers, citizens, and decision makers on a regular basis. Even for governments that have stellar reputations for decades of emphasis on performance management, promises to deliver timely information are often difficult to maintain.

We've often praised Virginia for its management practices and it still pays solid attention to strategic planning and provides a wealth of performance information on its Department of Planning and Budget website.[1] But the state's agencies vary substantially on how actively they maintain current data. On the plus side, in spring 2019, the Department of Social Services was able to report many of its measures through the second or third quarter of 2019. It showed that the placement of foster children with families, which hovered around 70 percent in 2007, was close to 82 percent for the first three quarters of 2019.[2]

On the other hand, the Virginia Economic Development Partnership's so-called annual reporting of the number of new jobs created by new and existing companies provided its last count as of

2016, even though notes on the website say the measure is active and that annual results for the fiscal year just ending are known after August 31 of each fiscal year.[3] Many Department of Health measures are updated only through 2015, partially due to dependence on federal data.[4]

Another disheartening issue with public displays of performance information is that the number of people who pay attention can be disappointingly low.

As Guenevere Knowles, associate director for performance management at the New York City Mayor's Office of Operations, told us, "We thought dashboards were going to help inform decisions. But I know that the tons of data that we put out doesn't get that many views." This is the ultimate governmental equivalent of trees falling in abandoned forests.[5]

New York is a city with a long history of performance management, a much-cited *Mayor's Management Report*, and a stellar office of data analysis. But in many other governments, performance management still falls short of penetrating most departments or of being supported by a strong infrastructure and needed resources.

In its Equipt to Innovate survey, Living Cities and *Governing* examined seven elements that make up a high-performing city, all relating either indirectly or directly to performance management.[6] The most recent report, released in June 2019, found cities were strong in strategic planning and in tracking performance measurements, but less than half of the cities surveyed had policies or ordinances to establish a performance management program (see figure 2.1). Fifty-five percent said they needed to increase use of evidence-based approaches when developing programs.[7]

In its 2018 brief on outcome monitoring, the Pew Charitable Trusts-MacArthur Results First team highlighted a disconnect between the data collected and reported by agencies and its use by decision makers. As the Results First report said, "State agencies frequently spend significant resources to collect and report performance data that may not always be useful to decision-makers. At the same time, policymakers may lack information they need to make important policy and funding decisions."[8]

Figure 2.1 Room for Improvement

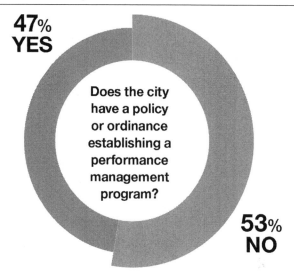

47%
YES

Does the city
have a policy
or ordinance
establishing a
performance
management
program?

53%
NO

How many cities say they have policies or ordinances establishing a performance
management program?
Credit: *Governing*, Equipt to Innovate Report, 2019

SUSTAINABILITY

Even when information has been gathered and utilized, sustaining these efforts can be difficult over time. Performance management systems take considerable effort, and even governments with strong performance reputations have seen activities ebb away as external events refocus attention or political newcomers abandon past initiatives and move on. There's nothing like a powerful hurricane to distract city leaders from perusing the latest measures about the parks system. Conversely, some governments that were doing the least twenty-five years ago are now leaders. This includes, for example, New Mexico, which we criticized in 1993 for having no performance measurements and minimal evaluations.[9] It is now one of the most innovative states in this field.

There is inevitably an ebb and flow of activity. Brent Stockwell, assistant city manager in Scottsdale, Arizona, started volunteering for the city's well-known organizational effectiveness unit in 1993, shortly after graduating from the University of Washington. He went to work for the city nine years later.

Although that effort ceased to exist, Scottsdale continued to measure performance through the years and periodically, the city participated in the ICMA[10] effort to compare performance across jurisdictions. But despite this tenacity, the budget office, where the responsibility for performance measurement was centered, found it difficult to get good information from the departments. As performance measurement information was filed with decreasing enthusiasm, the budget office's own attention to performance measurement faded away and they "pretty much abandoned the effort," Stockwell says.

In 2009, Stockwell was asked to reestablish the unit he had volunteered for sixteen years before. He looked into promising practices in other governments and carefully studied advice in the report put out by the National Performance Management Advisory Committee.[11] While action was slowed down somewhat by the aftermath of the Great Recession, under Stockwell's guidance, a variety of new processes were put in place. Now Scottsdale is once again regarded as one of the strongest cities in terms of its performance management efforts.

THE HUMAN ELEMENT

With all of the attention given to data and new technological capabilities, the absence of a focus on people can doom the most sophisticated efforts.

Gathering appropriate data starts the process, but the data itself does not easily shed light on the cause of problems.

© iStock/Getty Images Plus/Nastco

Todd Park, then federal chief technology officer, addressed this issue in a 2013 speech. "Data by itself is useless," he said at a federal Geographic Information System conference in Washington, DC. conference in Washington, DC. "You can't pour data on a broken bone and heal it. You can't pour data on the street and fix it. Data is only useful if it is applied for useful public benefit."[12]

Sherry Schoonover, deputy director of information technology and chief security officer in Topeka, Kansas, brings up the city's effort to cut back on code violations on properties. "We're trying to get the number down but is it not more important to identify and come up with ways of how to reduce the interaction between us and district court?" she asks. "What is the process and is there something that can be done? It's very difficult if you have an old lady who has mobility issues, she can't cut the grass, but she'll get cited for the grass being too tall."

It's a question, she says, of "how can we provide assistance, and not just about asking 'what are the numbers?' "

Inger Brinck, director of Results Washington, told us, "Our organization is focusing on being human centered, connecting the data with the people it impacts. Each of the dashboards has a summary of the issues but also a link and connection to a story that is a person who is impacted by this work. It helps us not to disconnect the work we're doing from the people who are benefiting."[13]

As Stephen Goldsmith, former Indianapolis mayor and former deputy mayor in New York City, has written, "human centered design principles use what data reveals as merely the first guideposts on the pathway to understanding the distinct profiles of individuals within a system—whether criminal justice, health care, transportation or any other area of governmental interest."[14]

DIFFERING PERSPECTIVES

There are sometimes tensions that stem from disagreements among practitioners with different points of view: program evaluators and others who seek to measure and improve performance.

Program evaluators maintain a rigorous approach that follows set standards of practice. The time that evaluations take can feel burdensome to practitioners who are looking for immediate answers to pressing problems.

On the other hand, managers seeking to measure and improve performance in central government offices or in agencies, approach their work without the kind of standardized rigor upon which evaluators insist. These performance and innovation chiefs, data analysts, and process improvement specialists come to their positions from a wide variety of backgrounds and different levels of education and experience and have no preordained set of credentials.

One other distinction between the two is that performance management, as practiced by a variety of government practitioners, can increasingly be accomplished on a close-to-real-time basis, by regularly measuring the results of programs, analyzing data, and introducing improvements.

In 2019, Mathematica Policy Research conducted a podcast featuring Katherine Klosek, director of applied research at the Center for Government Excellence (GovEx) at Johns Hopkins University. She summed up this distinction: "There's this natural tension that's arising where decision makers need timely data points to indicate what to do almost on a daily basis, (but) rigorous policy analysis takes time. So, there's this tension between wanting a really robust body of evidence and needing performance metrics to indicate what to do and where (to) invest right now."[15]

Don Moynihan, McCourt chair at the McCourt School of Public Policy at Georgetown University, has written extensively about performance management and observes that there has been a longtime split in professional approaches. As he told us, "You could look at the history of program evaluation and performance measurement as a cautionary tale of two children who were brought up in the same house but were raised by different tribes and aren't so friendly with one another."[16]

Whatever the training and perspective of the players who contribute to improved performance, the approaches appear to be most effective when they complement each other. Performance management should be a state or citywide effort involving multiple individuals in many different roles.

Says Stockwell, "It's not 100 percent of anyone's job, but part of everyone's job."

3

Benefits

■ ■ ■

WHY SHOULD YOU BOTHER to read a book that covers the ins and outs and the in-betweens of performance management? Obviously, if an understanding of performance management doesn't have value to practitioners, elected officials, and academics, there's no point in reading on.

This is not a problem. Multiple examples show the success of performance management efforts and the often-unrecognized improvements in the way services and programs are delivered.

Steven Rathgeb Smith is executive director of the American Political Science Association. His early work experiences in the mid-1970s involved residential treatment facilities in New York City and Rhode Island, and then at a Massachusetts agency focused on individuals with developmental disabilities. Each of these agencies received funding from their respective state or local governments.

"Back then, nobody was paying attention to performance or accountability," he says, "Initially, nobody was tracking outcomes or had much of a performance expectation. It was trusting the agencies to do what was in the best interest of the clients and there were lots of stories of child welfare agencies where the services weren't that good." Beyond that, elected officials had a propensity to claim that the only performance measure they cared about was to be found in the jurisdiction's ballot boxes on election day. Getting reelected was the only metric they needed to claim success.

"Today, the increased attention to outcomes and evaluation has definitely improved services over the long term. The greater focus on performance management and evidence-based practice and policy making has, in my view, had many benefits in the way services are provided."

EXHIBIT A: MONTGOMERY COUNTY

For many years, Montgomery County, Maryland, whose population of over one million people live near-in to Washington, DC, has had a performance focus. That's just accelerated in the last few years with the addition of online mapping tools and seeking out ways to further embed its performance culture throughout the county. This has helped to dramatically increase productive collaborations with the nonprofit community and has advanced the county's ability to ensure that the county administration and community stakeholders—as well as other government partners—can have conversations with the same set of information.[1]

A mainstay of Montgomery's efforts, CountyStat, started a little more than ten years ago. One of its first initiatives focused on pedestrian safety. Data analysis pinpointed the actions needed to prevent injuries and save pedestrian lives. Follow-up data showed the county where it was successful and where it had to redouble safety efforts and think more strategically.

Part of the project involved targeting selected school routes where more accidents than average had occurred. To protect pedestrians, the county stepped up traffic enforcement. It made a variety of changes in traffic signals and in road and sidewalk design, installed better signage, and gave pedestrians the ability to push a button to start lights flashing when they entered a crosswalk. (This has apparently been effective in Montgomery County, in contrast to other cities where similar transit buttons seem to be connected to a block of wood someplace.) An education campaign was also launched in schools and neighborhoods, as county data showed that driver and pedestrian fault was shared. (In 2009, drivers were at fault in 46 percent of cases, pedestrians in 42 percent, with the rest undetermined.[2])

In the three years before the initiative there were forty-eight car–pedestrian collisions in the eleven school neighborhoods that were targeted. In the three years after, there were seven.

One more interesting result from the county's pedestrian safety efforts: It uncovered the fact that, based on 2012 data, 29 percent of accidents occurred in parking lots. This was a problem that had gone practically unnoticed. Because parking lots are mostly privately owned, the county could not turn to the kinds of enforcement or physical improvements it had made on streets and sidewalks, but it was able to embark on a big education campaign. "We had to do it all through public information. We partnered with the Public Information Office to do an awareness campaign about keeping your head up in a parking lot whether you are a driver or a pedestrian," says David Gottesman, CountyStat manager.

The county's pedestrian safety program, now tagged with the well-known Vision Zero[3] label, continues to explore and analyze data to help pinpoint areas of the county where pedestrian car collisions are more frequent and when they are most likely to occur.[4]

A CATALOG OF BENEFITS

Montgomery County is just one particularly strong piece of evidence of the benefits of performance management. Through the remainder of this chapter, you'll find a series of examples from a variety of sources that show the different kinds of improvements that have been achieved with the help of performance measurement, benchmarking, data analysis, process improvement, program evaluation, and all of the other tools that are used to manage performance.

San Jose

Although there are impediments to using performance management to influence budgeting decisions, as described in chapter 6, there are many instances in which fiscal decisions are influenced by the data collected and analyzed by executive branch performance managers, evaluators, and appointed or elected auditors.

In San Jose, California, the city auditor's office publishes an annual services report, which strategically comes out in December, right before January budget deliberations.[5]

The report includes performance results by department as well as the results of an annual citizen survey. What differentiates the San Jose report from many other performance documents is its emphasis on trends. While the report focuses on performance measures for the previous year, it also includes multiple trend tables showing the measures and what they reveal about city services and problems over the last ten years.

"With the long trends you can really see what's happening," says recently retired city auditor Sharon Erickson. Coming out right before budget deliberations also helps keep it front and center when elected officials and their staffs decide what to do with the city's programs. "It shows the major issues that we need to address in the coming year and the council begins their budget deliberations using that information," she says.

For example, the December 2018 report showed that the city's pavement condition earned a 67 out of 100 rating and that some city streets were so worn that expensive repairs were needed to keep them from "deteriorating rapidly." Just 14 percent of residents rated street repair as good or excellent (see figure 3.1). By comparison, 39 percent rated city services generally as good or excellent.[6]

The street data hit home with the City Council (see figure 3.2) and it fully funded the street repair program in 2019. This included repaving 88 miles of major streets and 200 miles of smaller streets. (The report's ongoing highlighting of street repair issues also may have helped to lead to the approval of a November 2018 ballot measure, in which 69 percent of San Jose residents said yes to a $650 million bond package dedicated both to improving streets and disaster response.)

Minnesota

We have often repeated a basic principle we learned from the Urban Institute's Harry Hatry, who has strongly influenced the practice of performance measurement over the last decades. As he told us back in

Figure 3.1 Resident Survey

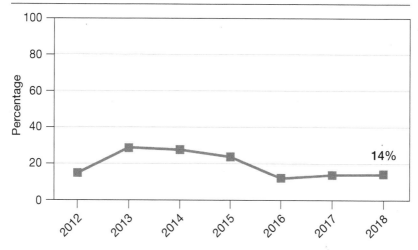

Percentage of San Jose residents rating street repair as "excellent" or "good."
A survey of residents in San Jose has consistently demonstrated low satisfaction with streets.
Credit: Office of the City Auditor, San Jose

the early 2000s, "overall data hides the real information. Breaking it out is the only way to make performance data useful for managing. If you're looking at street cleanliness, you should know where the dirty streets are."

According to Myron Frans, commissioner of Minnesota's Department of Management and Budget, "It's an expectation [among policymakers] that we disaggregate our data, especially with regards to racial, socioeconomic, and geographic factors. Things can look great in the aggregate, but not so great when you drill down. We break out the data so that we can improve the services we provide."[7]

This approach has been a powerful tool for managers who have been intent on improving the diversity of the state's workforce. This was a focus area during the administration of Governor Mark Dayton and continues to be for current governor Tim Walz. When Frans joined the Dayton administration in 2011, the first year of Governor Dayton's first term, he says there was demographic information on the workforce, but it was not being closely tracked or used to make policy and human resource decisions.

Figure 3.2 Funding Needed to Fix Poor, Failed, and Overdue Roads

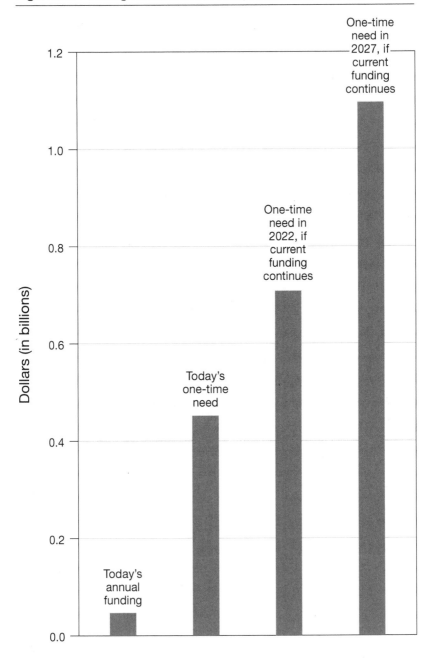

Information from the San Jose City Auditor tells the City Council how much repair costs mount when ignored.
Credit: Office of the City Auditor, San Jose

"We started earnestly looking at this and then we implemented really big changes in the hiring process," says Frans. That meant eliminating outdated unnecessary qualifications that were keeping people who were able to do state jobs from getting them. It also meant using a statewide executive recruiter, setting up hiring panels, and recently hiring a chief inclusion officer. An important part of the diversity effort is to talk about it in multiple parts of the state. As Frans sees it, "When you target the data and then use it to implement programs, you can have a great effect."

In the Department of Management and Budget (MMB), people of color represented 10 percent of employees eight years ago. That has now grown to 15.5 percent. For the state workforce, racial and ethnic minorities were 8.1 percent of the workforce at the beginning of 2011. When Governor Walz took over in January 2019, they represented 13.6 percent. During that same period, the percentage of employees with disabilities rose from 4.6 percent to 7.1 percent. Those percentages are continuing to grow.

Minnesota is also learning from breakdowns of data in its education system. For example, student housing information shows that 8,700 students in Minnesota experienced homelessness during the 2017 to 2018 school year. Mixing that data with school test information reveals that only one in four third graders who experienced homelessness were proficient in reading—37 percent lower than low-income peers. Homelessness also increased chronic absenteeism. Research has shown that low third grade reading scores appear to lead to diminished academic success in future grades,[8] with early chronic absenteeism contributing to elevated high school dropout rates.[9]

Guided by the data, Minnesota created its "Homework Starts with Home" program, which provides rent and housing assistance to families who lack housing stability. "By targeting homeless assistance and housing assistance, we've seen this can improve educational outcomes," says Frans. So far, the program has helped 375 families and the governor has proposed doubling the money put into the program and the number of families served in 2020.

Wisconsin

Not only can analysis of the data derived through performance management systems help to improve and build confidence in the viability of individual programs, but it can be equally useful to accomplish just the opposite. When there's ample proof that policy is not having the success that was hoped for, performance information can help to avoid moving full speed on unproductive paths.

For example, if a child is placed in foster care, should his natural parents be asked to pay child support? The Institute for Research on Poverty at the University of Wisconsin used data to study this issue and found that requiring child support was counterproductive in that it lengthened the time spent in foster care because of the economic burden it put on families.[10]

Data analysis showed that a $100 monthly increase in child support resulted in 6.6 more months in foster care. (What's more, child support for foster care only provided about 3 percent of the actual cost of the care.)

Research helped to convince policymakers to scale back "the requirement to pay child support for foster care, with the goal of increasing the number of family reunifications and positive outcomes."[11]

Indiana

There are plenty of barriers to data sharing, but they are beginning to fall and the benefits for governments that have succeeded in melding data are easy to see. A growing number of local governments and states are taking steps to share data across a cadre of agencies to facilitate a holistic approach to performance management.

Indiana's Management and Performance Hub (MPH) became an official Indiana department in 2017. The hub's emphasis on data sharing has been a potent weapon in the state's fight against the opioid epidemic. The approach has included the use of dashboards to inform the public, managers, and decision makers of important dimensions of the opioid problem—related emergency room visits, opioid deaths, and prescription information, for example. But the dashboards, while useful, are essentially a means of effectively communicating information, not the key element in using it.

"The work that sets Indiana apart from other states isn't the dashboards but work in linking all the datasets together," according to Tim George, policy director at the office of Indiana governor Eric Holcomb. "This allows us to evaluate the risk profiles for various individuals."

The state's opiate work involved data-sharing among ten partner agencies. Combined data about where opiate-related problems are occurring was used to create a heat map that has helped the state consider the best places to locate treatment facilities. This also provides local governments with detailed information that can be used by law enforcement and health services, minimizing the need for each town, city, or county to develop its own data initiatives. The MPH annual report estimates these led to a 5 percent reduction in opioid-related visits to emergency departments and a 10 percent drop in calls for medics to administer the overdose reversal drug Naloxone.[12]

Denver, Colorado

The multiaward-winning Denver Peak Academy has now trained thousands of Denver employees to improve management using process improvement techniques inspired by the Lean Business Management Method.

These performance improvement efforts are often focused on small goals with modest financial improvement—like the wastewater utility suggestion to use first-class mail instead of certified mail to alert residents of an upcoming lien on their property—a change that saved the city $46,000 annually.[13] But even small savings, multiplied by hundreds of different improvements, add up.

By August 2017, the Denver Peak Academy had saved the city $22.5 million since its 2011 beginning, according to the mayor's office. In those years, 6,500 employees had been through the Academy and had come up with 2,300 innovations.

Some of its achievements:[14]

- Saving $7 million by strengthening the city fleet of vehicles.
- Obtaining a business license in twenty minutes rather than two hours.

- Receiving food assistance in twenty-four hours rather than six days.
- Reducing the length of stay at an animal shelter to seven days, down from fourteen.
- Making a visit to the Department of Motor Vehicles twenty minutes instead of the eighty it may have been in years past.
- Acquiring top talent for new hires in sixty days rather than eighty-five, with a goal of forty-five days by end of year.

King County, Washington

King County, Washington—the thirteenth-largest county in the United States—encapsulates many benefits that come from comparing how services and funding affect different demographic groups. It has used this kind of data disaggregation to focus on one of its principle goals—achieving racial equity within its boundaries. This includes its county seat, the City of Seattle, which often scores high on comparative measures of its quality of life.

But King County carefully tracks quality of life measures, showing not just the disparity among different demographic groups in Seattle but over the county's 2,037 square miles and across its 2.2 million population. Looking across the county, "life expectancy ranges from 74 years to 87 years, smoking ranges from 5 percent to 20 percent, and frequent mental distress ranges from 4 percent to 14 percent," according to the 2015 Equity and Social Justice Strategic Plan, which was formed using input from six hundred county employees and one hundred local organizations.[15]

Armed with that kind of information, King County has become widely acknowledged to be one of the nation's local governments to move furthest ahead in developing a full "plan-do-check-act" system for performance management.

The data, broken down in a variety of ways in King County, show common problems of inequity. And that gives the county the knowledge base necessary to implement aggressive solutions, including a redirection of funding, so that services can be targeted to where they'll have the biggest effect.

Specific programs include King County's Best Starts for Kids, with its focus on early intervention, and the county's determined effort to provide integrated services for physical health, mental health, and substance abuse rather than separate siloed health services.

King County's approach to solving problems has benefited from years of exploration of productive and less productive performance management efforts. We asked Michael Jacobson, deputy director of performance and strategy in King County, what was the most distinguishing factor of King County's approach. "We are trying to build a system," he said, "that includes planning performance management, performance oversight, management review, and improving the use of performance data in the budget process. We're trying to infuse all of that into a full performance management system."

He added that the county also uses tools inspired by the Lean philosophy and approach[16] and it recently launched a public reporting platform to show progress (as well as lack of progress) on its equity and social justice plan. In 2019, it won the Organizational Leadership Award from the Center of Accountability and Performance, part of the American Society for Public Administration.[17]

CASE STUDY

New Orleans: Shock Therapy

When Mitch Landrieu became mayor of New Orleans in 2010, the city was suffering from the aftermath of Hurricane Katrina. There were an estimated forty-three thousand properties that had been abandoned and were decaying (see photo 3.1). Abandoned properties became magnets for crime and the devastating impact on neighborhoods resulted in property values declining. Abandoned properties attracted drug dealers.

New Orleans' initial approach to achieving Mayor Landrieu's goal was to develop a Stat process, dubbed BlightStat, that was similar to Baltimore's CityStat model. Data was tracked to see whether inspections were keeping up with targets. The men and women responsible for putting blighted properties on the road to demolishment or salvation were held accountable for their results.

Although the performance improved, as measured by the Stat system, "the rate of improvement wasn't sustainable," says Oliver Wise, whom Landrieu had appointed director of the New Orleans Office of Performance and Accountability. In addition, the ability to utilize inspections to demolish or fix properties to make improvements was slow.

New Orleans Blight.
Credit: City of New Orleans' Department of Code Enforcement

Wise describes the New Orleans Stat System as "shock therapy" for a very dysfunctional government.

While this kind of performance measurement was the first tool to attack the city's blight problem, just measuring progress toward targets did not engender sustainable solutions to accelerate blight removal. The performance team turned to intense analysis of all the data available to them to better understand what was needed to make genuine progress.

Although the big first moves the city made were to increase the frequency of inspections and to purchase more bulldozers to eliminate unredeemable properties, data analysis showed that more needed to be done. Increasing inspections, alone, was just the beginning. It was up to an administrative law judge to render a property as blighted and then that information could be used to make the decisions that would lead to either renovating or destroying the property. "We needed to build legal capacity . . . a complete end-to-end view of the code enforcement process. That was a total pivot that was not at all in the mayor's original strategy," Wise says.

The new approach changed the performance team's relationship with departments more generally.

Wise provides the details of a stellar example in the fire department, which had problems meeting its performance targets for response time.

In November 2014, a major fire occurred where five people, including three children died. The house did not have smoke detectors. The fire chief wanted to be much more aggressive about prevention. Although the department was willing to give out free detectors, few people were asking for them.

The city decided it was important to reach out, with the offer of free detectors, in a targeted fashion. In the right homes, the logic held, property damage and personal injuries from fires could be prevented. The performance team created an app that predicted places that were most in need of smoke alarms. "The fire department was able to go out in a very strategic precise way to provide the service to the neighborhoods most in need," Wise says. These tended to be places where elderly residents and children lived. "That's the population that is most likely to die if there is a fire in the house."

While it's difficult to prove cause and effect, after this program was established, there was a fire in a house that had recently received free smoke detectors and eleven people were able to escape. No one died.[18]

That demonstrated the value of this program to the fire department, which became far more invested in what the performance team was doing. What's more, unlike the original Stat system, which was rooted in accountability—and potentially fostered distaste for what was seen by some as a "gotcha" exercise—it became clear that the performance unit had assets that could help add value.

Recalls Wise, "It was a boon to the fire chief's career and his standing and his positioning with fire chiefs around the country."

Performance shops are in a much different place now than ten years ago, says Wise. They began with an accountability orientation with their work focused on catching underperformers and on identifying the size and dimensions of problems. But as time has passed, the availability of data has exploded and the technology to access that data has gotten much better. The result? Data are increasingly used to improve and not just measure performance.

4

History

■ ■ ■

EVERY GENERATION IN GOVERNMENT tends to believe it has discovered a new management wheel. Old-timers in the field of performance management often cluck to one another about how they experimented with many of today's "innovations" twenty or thirty years earlier.

The reality is that current work in performance management—though often described as new—has roots that are a century old.

This may be an overstatement, but the biblical chapter Ecclesiastes was pretty much on the mark in the words, "What has been will be again, what has been done, will be done again,"

Groundwork that has culminated in many of today's public sector performance management efforts dates back to the turn of the twentieth century. These tended to be launched by prominent individuals in the private sector such as John D. Rockefeller, Andrew Carnegie, and E. H. Harriman, who started the New York Bureau of Municipal Research in 1905, which led a few years later to a new Training School for Public Service.[1]

They were motivated by a desire to wipe out government corruption, save money, and make services more efficient and effective. Their successful fight to drive out political corruption spurred a new breed of reformers to work within government to improve service and strive for better results.

Ralph Blumenthal, a retired *New York Times* reporter, has been uncovering multiple past management initiatives, as he has sorted through seven hundred previously stored and forgotten boxes of government papers housed at Baruch College of the City University of New York, where he is a distinguished lecturer in the Baruch library.

In these boxes, he found the stories of management heroes like Luther Halsey Gulick,[2] who led the Bureau of Municipal Research, which later became the Institute of Public Administration, bringing the new science of efficient, honest, and transparent government to New York and multiple municipalities.

"He was a mastermind. It's not a well-known story, but he brought the whole process of performance management into government," says Blumenthal.

In the first two decades of the twentieth century, "budget exhibits" began appearing around the country dedicated to improving government performance, heightening revenue and spending transparency, and connecting spending to results.

In New York in 1911, hundreds of citizens lined up to hear lectures and view posters that conveyed information about government spending in a very similar fashion to today's web pages.

Other cities to jump on the budget exhibit concept were St. Louis, Missouri, and Spokane, Washington. Posters highlighted wasteful spending (see figure 4.1), benchmarked performance against city peers, explained budget concepts, and illustrated the relationship between spending and outcomes. In one poster, a list of urban investments was placed adjacent to the negative results that would occur without them. For example, more spending on playgrounds and children's libraries would lead to fewer vagrants and beggars.

In the second decade of the century, budget exhibits spread to many major cities, but as the posters on display sometimes became strident, the exhibits also drew detractors who complained the exhibits were too political and not scientific. By the 1920s, the budget exhibit movement had become passé.[3]

Although this means of disseminating good management practices faded, performance management initiatives didn't disappear. Rather, they accelerated as the century progressed.

Figure 4.1

A GRAPHIC METHOD OF SHOWING THE MONEY COST OF LEAKY FAUCETS.

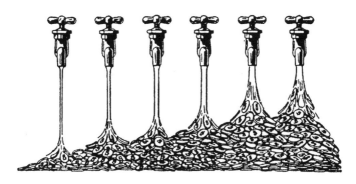

Under Average Water Rates and Pressures This is the Way That Leaks
Run into Money.

Each 1-64 inch leak wastes 2 gallons per hour and costs   .   .   .   1c per day
Each 1-32 inch leak wastes 8 gallons per hour and costs   .   .   .   5c per day
Each 1-16 inch leak wastes 34 gallons per hour and costs   .   .   .   21c per day
Each 1-8 inch leak wastes 137 gallons per hour and costs   .   .   .   86c per day
Each 1-4 inch leak wastes 514 gallons per hour and costs   .   . $3.21 per day
Each 1-2 inch leak wastes 2057 gallons per hour and costs .   . $12.84 per day

For example, the first of a series of International City/County Management Association articles on ways to improve local government performance appeared in *Public Management* magazine in 1932.[4] Among the types of articles featured was one about various standards for appraising programs.

In 1954, Peter Drucker, sometimes known as the founder of modern management, published a treatise, "Management by Objectives," which became a major influence on both business and government. Around the same time, business reengineering and the quality management movement were gaining adherents, first in Japan, then throughout the world.

One of Drucker's oft-quoted maxims relates directly to today's work in performance management: "Most discussions of decision making assume that only senior executives make decisions or that only senior executives' decisions matter. This is a dangerous mistake."

PROGRESS AT THE STATE LEVEL

After decades in which federal budgeting concentrated on avoiding fraud and making sure the books balanced, the notion that better management could result in better budgets emerged at the federal level in the 1950s. The advent of the federal government's thrust to so-called planning-programming-budgeting in the 1960s helped to escalate the use of performance measurement in the United States.[5]

State activity paralleled the federal government, where "program budgeting" was implemented in the 1960s and 1970s so that resources could be linked with spending results. At the time, it was a struggle even to convince cities, counties, and states that measuring what they did was an important part of government. Measuring results was frightening. "There was resistance to outcome or effectiveness evaluation," says Harry Hatry, now a senior fellow at the Urban Institute and one of the most influential forces in performance management from the 1960s to today. "Managers were concerned that you'd provide the media more ammunition to get them," he says. That wasn't necessarily a canard, but a handful of pioneers in the states advanced the idea that the benefits of performance management outweighed the political risks of transparency.

Minnesota's first stab (of many) at tying budgets to performance occurred in 1969 when the legislature mandated that agencies present future budgets, with attention to programs and what they were supposed to accomplish. This substituted for the more traditional approach in which dollars were allocated based on preordained expenditures for broad "objects of expense," such as repairs, salaries, or travel.[6]

In the 1970s, a handful of other states began tying their spending to performance. These included Alabama, which passed its Budget Management Act, requiring agencies to "write strategic plans and program objectives and report on them quarterly."[7] In Hawaii, the legislature passed a comprehensive performance measurement bill in 1970 that led to agency strategic plans, goal-setting, intense analysis, and performance budgeting, all accompanied by training for managers in adopting this performance-oriented culture.

The effort to professionalize legislatures took off in the 1970s as well, led by the Eagleton Institute of Politics at Rutgers University and its much-admired director Alan Rosenthal. One result was an increase in nonpartisan staff and a new emphasis on legislative research and evaluation, exemplified in the 1973 creation of Mississippi's Performance Evaluation and Expenditure Review Committee.

The 1970s also saw an increase in sunset laws that required legislative assessment of programs so that those that had outstayed their usefulness could be ended. In 1977, Tennessee passed a sunset law, which was designed to review programs and—if there was ample evidence that they were not effective—to defund them.

The job of assessing programs fell to the Tennessee audit office. But there was an obstacle. The audit office was manned by dozens of certified public accountants who knew a lot about auditing the state's finances, but little about how to evaluate a program. One small-scale effort to help bridge this gap was to hire an extraordinarily tall, young social worker with a political science degree who started out analyzing and evaluating programs and was soon in charge of a new kind of auditing staff that focused on how programs worked rather than on financial and compliance issues.

"There were zero intellectual tools to do the work, but I had carte blanche to do what I wanted to do and I was good at it," says Mark Funkhouser, who became one of the leaders of the new performance auditing profession, edited the *Local Government Auditing Quarterly*, and later became auditor of Kansas City, mayor of Kansas City, publisher of *Governing* magazine, and director of the Governing Institute.

"We said we were doing program evaluation until we went to an audit conference at GAO that was talking about audit standards.[8] I coauthored a piece in *Government Finance Review* that made the argument that this should be called performance auditing."

Slow progression in the 1980s saw five other states developing performance budgeting laws, with twenty-six more joining in during the 1990s.[9] If you add in states with administrative rules dictating a connection between the budget and performance information, all but three states had some type of performance budgeting requirement by 1998,[10] although many of these efforts were ineffective or barely enforced.

Then there was the Total Quality Management movement (TQM), fostered in the 1980s and early 1990s after the publication of W. Edwards Demming's book *Out of the Crisis* in 1982. Although the phrase is infrequently used today, TQM was not dissimilar from current work aimed at continuous improvement in the quality of services and products based on data, employee input, the development of improvement teams, and measurement of performance.

TQM attracted followers in federal, state, and local governments. A GAO briefing report in 1992 found most federal organizational units were applying some TQM principles.[11]

OUR RINGSIDE VIEW

Our ringside view of performance management began in 1990 when we had an audacious idea—spurred by the number of governors who were then talking about running their states like businesses—of comparing all fifty states on their capacity in various management practices for *Financial World* magazine.

As we started making phone calls to figure out how to do this, we talked with Jay Fountain, who was leading the Governmental Accounting Standards Board's (GASB) exploration into the possibility of adding performance measurement information to financial reporting standards.

He easily convinced us of the importance for governments of knowing the results of their spending and reporting on this information to citizens. We talked with John Kamensky at the GAO, who shared with us his explorations of performance measurement in New Zealand, Australia, Canada, and the United Kingdom, all places that were ahead of the United States in measuring the results of what they did. Harry Hatry, at the Urban Institute, educated us still further.

After our first seat-of-the-pants effort to evaluate state governments, the next year we did the same with the thirty largest cities. Between 1990 and 2008, we were involved in various projects that sought to evaluate states, cities, and counties (and briefly federal agencies) on their use of performance information. The Government Performance Project, which was launched in 1997 and funded by the Pew Charitable Trusts, had a federal component that was published in *Government Executive*, and a state, city, and county component that was published in *Governing* magazine.[12]

During that period, we witnessed multiple changes in the field. Through the 1990s, Managing for Results conferences, held by the LBJ School at the University of Texas in Austin, biannually brought together hundreds of enthusiastic local and state practitioners of new performance measurement and management initiatives; the GASB ran training sessions through the country, although it faced opposition from city and state membership organizations that were concerned that the standards-setting body had overstepped its role and that its explorations would ultimately necessitate auditing of performance measures, a potentially overwhelming task (see case study on page 38).

FEDERAL ADVANCES

For the federal government, the 1990s were also a time of huge growth in performance measurement and management activity. This included the passage of the Government Performance and Results Act in 1993 and The National Performance Review, a management initiative of the Bill Clinton presidential administration. Led by Vice President Al Gore, the review used internal teams to uncover and implement ways of improving government performance. The effort was heavily influenced by David Osborne and Ted Gaebler's best-selling book, *Reinventing Government*, which was published in 1993, and was reportedly bedside reading for the new president in the early days of his administration.

The National Performance Review ended with the Clinton administration, and the George W. Bush presidency instituted its Program Assessment Rating Tool, which identified one thousand programs in the federal government, with each program scored on effectiveness, on a sliding scale with "effective" at the top, and "ineffective" at the bottom. A traffic light system of "red," "yellow," and "green" marks alerted website visitors to whether programs were meeting targets or not.

Relying too heavily on the percentage of targets attained was a big mistake, according to Shelley Metzenbaum, who was the Obama-appointed associate director of performance and personnel management at the Office of Management and Budget from 2009 to 2013. Under her leadership, the administration dropped the emphasis on meeting targets and added strategic performance goals and

---

Box 4.1 | Building the Federal Performance Infrastructure

The last thirty years have seen several key steps taken in the federal government to build up a performance management infrastructure.

1993—The Government Performance and Results Act (GPRA) required federal agencies to engage in strategic planning, and to report on their own performance. Initial reviews of the act cited many benefits, including a major increase in federal performance information. A major disappointment, however, has stemmed from the limited use of GPRA information for improving performance, a problem noted in multiple GAO reports.

2010—The GPRA Modernization Act added several important components to the 1990s act in an effort to increase its impact on performance. This included the identification of high-priority goals and goal leaders. Performance improvement officers were put in place in each agency and a Performance Improvement Council was formed so they could regularly meet together. GAO reports about the use of performance information continue to be disappointing.

2016–2018—The bipartisan Evidence-Based Policymaking Commission Act of 2016 created a commission to develop a strategy promoting the use of data to build capacity for using evidence in creating, managing, sustaining, or taking down government programs.

The Commission's report, released in 2017, spurred the 115th Congress to pass the "Foundations of Evidence-Based Policymaking Act of 2018" just before adjourning in December of that year. The act requires that agencies have chief data officers and evaluation officers and that they have an evaluation policy and evidence-building plans.

---

cross-agency priority goals, emphasizing the trends that showed the direction in which government was moving.

Many of the Barack Obama administration initiatives have been continued by the Donald Trump administration, which has left performance issues largely in the hands of Office of Management and Budget senior staff.

UPS AND DOWNS

Through the eighteen years in which we evaluated state and local efforts at government performance management, we learned not to praise governments too quickly for their enthusiastic plunge into the field or the individual approaches they took.

While the effort has generally been improving, few governments, if any, really travel a straight line forward. Alabama and Hawaii, which were innovators in performance measurement in the 1970s, were laggards when we looked in 1995, earning a D+ and a D, respectively, in our "managing for results" assessment.[13]

For the purposes of this book, we've used boxfuls of material from our Financial World work and the GPP to track the progress of performance management at all levels of government through 2008. In the 1990s and early 2000s, Maine's love–hate relationship with performance measurement and strategic planning took the state on a roller-coaster ride in which measures were required, then dropped, then required again.

Briefly, even the reference to performance measurement was banned from budget discussions, in the same way as smoking in public buildings is now. A state senator in 2008 noted the effect of term limits on the effort. "You had a group of legislators that's very committed to performance budgeting and put it in place," Maine's state senator Peggy Rotundo told the GPP. "Then with the new people rotating through, you didn't have the same level of understanding. It sort of lost steam over a period of time."[14]

© iStock/Getty Images Plus/Lessimol

Even governments that showed a steady interest in performance management across the decades tried out multiple different approaches, tossing out one and bringing in another, much like tissues in a box. In Minnesota, where agencies had long been reporting performance measurement in their budgets, the legislature decided in 1993 to require annual performance reports as well. In 1998, the legislature repealed that requirement.

The performance reports were supposed to ratchet up clear agency information, lead to better measures, and generate useful conversations with legislative committees. "But it was a challenge to try to train agencies about what this was all about and make them feel that it was something worth doing," says Joel Alter, director of special reviews for Minnesota's office of the legislative auditor.

Worse yet, even when the agencies bought in, some legislative committees did not, leading agencies to feel that their efforts were a waste of time. "I could have envisioned a scenario where it all played out better. If we just had enough time to work with agencies, we could have gotten to a point where the measures were better, and the data were better," says Alter.

Other initiatives emerged in the 1990s, including the alliteratively appealing Minnesota Milestones. It was launched early in the Gov. Arne Carlson administration and sought to chart the large societal impact desired by the governor. The goals were far reaching and extended beyond anything that an agency could possibly accomplish on even a medium- or long-term basis. A sample of goals: "Our children will not live in poverty" and "Minnesotans will be healthy."

While the milestones drew national attention in Governor Carlson's first term, by the mid-to-late 1990s, both internal and external focus had dimmed. When wrestling star Jesse Ventura became Minnesota governor in 1999, he abandoned the milestones and set up his own approach to performance management. His "Big Plan" used multiple citizen advisory groups to come up with twenty-nine initiatives attached to topics like "self-sufficient people" and "healthy vital communities."

While individual states and cities often go through multiple different versions of performance measurement and management approaches, by the time the Government Performance Project was winding to a close, our conclusions about progress were largely optimistic.

The field of performance auditing was one in which we saw growing interest. The Association of Local Government Auditors, founded in 1989 and devoted to performance rather than financial auditing, saw its membership grow from 167 members in 1990 to 524 by the end of the decade.[15] State legislative performance audits expanded also in the 1990s and by 2008, performance auditing of some sort was taking place in four out of five states.

By 2008, strategic planning had become a routine, accepted part of government and it was the norm for states to have either strategic plans for the entity as a whole or (more commonly) collections of agency plans. This was true in only half of the states in 1999. In 2008, just nine states were weak in both statewide and agency planning.[16]

ALTERNATE APPROACHES

States and local governments have continued to travel a bumpy road, with resource issues thwarting individual performance management efforts, particularly during the Great Recession and its long aftermath. With money tight, a series of worthwhile research and evaluation programs at the state level were cut back and others were defunded entirely by their legislatures, including the Kentucky Long-Term Policy Research Center, and the Oregon Progress Board (see box, page 45).

Various new methods continue to pop up, gaining adherents and then fading out of view. Charlotte, North Carolina, pioneered the "balanced score card" approach, which provides an organized way to establish linkages between internal measures, including those targeted to customer service and efficiency, and broader strategic vision or objectives. That city has been a stalwart adherent for decades, but elsewhere that movement has dissipated over time.

Zero-based budgeting comes and goes and comes again. This approach shifts away from far more common incremental budgeting traditions, in which budgets start out from a base that was set the previous year and are then adjusted to accommodate new programs or inflationary growth. In contrast, zero-based budgeting regards each budget as a fresh start, with all spending considered anew in each budgetary period. Jimmy Carter utilized zero-based budgeting as governor of Georgia in the 1970s, then pushed for the approach at the federal level when he became president. Zero-based budgeting was utilized for a while, but then abandoned early in President Ronald Reagan's first term, when it was labeled as too complicated and time-consuming.[17] In 2019, New Orleans has just started reforming its budget by trying out zero-based budgeting,

Pay for Performance initiatives in which employees or teams receive financial rewards for superior work, have sprung up in some jurisdictions but can be hobbled by economic downturns that cancel out the ability of governments to really come through with meaningful remuneration. They also generate criticism based on questions of subjectivity and fairness and are often opposed by unions.

In recent years, there has been a lot of talk about Pay-for-Success programs. But these efforts to get investors to take on the risk of program innovation have not yet recorded a lot of victories and the movement appears to be dying down.

One of the most electrifying approaches in the last three decades was started in the New York City police department by Police Commissioner William Bratton in 1995. CompStat aggressively utilized crime reporting data to pinpoint spikes in crime, with an emphasis on analysis, regular meetings to discuss data and trends, quick deployment of resources, and the assignment of individual responsibility for crime reduction. It spawned the Stat (for statistics) movement, with CompStat in New York focused on reducing crime rates, followed by others like CitiStat and StateStat in Baltimore and Maryland adding to the growing Stat reputation and its spread to multiple jurisdictions around the country and the world.

But the Stat movement was rough on participants and often generated a workload—and meeting load—that was hard to maintain. It now appears to be morphing into a gentler, more collaborative approach to data analysis and problem-solving (see chapter 8).

Sometimes external funding sources can galvanize a movement, as the Alfred P. Sloan Foundation did with its funding of performance reporting initiatives in the 1990s.

Of course, external funding can also be uncertain, at best. Just ask leaders of any organization that relies on sponsors, how secure they feel their jobs will be in two or three years. When the Sloan Foundation shifted its focus away from performance reporting, programs that had depended on those dollars dissolved. For example, a grant from Sloan enabled the Association of Government Accountants to start its Certificate of Achievement in Service Efforts & Accomplishments Reporting program in 2003, providing local entities a way to get input and strive for different levels of achievement based on the way they reported performance information. But, in the words of many a movie studio, Sloan decided to "take a different direction," and the program died around 2013.

More recent philanthropic examples include the Laura and John Arnold Foundation's policy lab support and its grants focused on evidence-based policy, and the Pew-MacArthur Results First initiative, which began in 2010 to help states and counties build successful programs by encouraging cost-benefit analysis and the use of evidence drawn from evaluations of past program results.[18]

Currently, one of the most active funders of performance programs has been the Bloomberg Philanthropies through its support for government innovation and its emphasis on data and evidence in the "What Works Cities" initiative, which is made up of five separate partner organizations, including Results for America, the lead organization. (For more about the What Works Cities resource, see appendix A for our list of helpful sources.)

One of the partners in "What Works Cities" is the Center for Government Excellence at Johns Hopkins University. Since 2015, it has worked with 140 mid size cities, training them in the use of a wide variety of tools to help use data and technology more effectively, employ behavioural economics, and improve performance analytics. An additional benefit for participants is the informal network that has formed among the cities, which regularly share ideas, problems, accomplishments, and innovations with each other.

For these and other cities, as well as states and counties, significant focus has been placed in recent years on accelerating the use of data to solve specific identifiable problems in programs as opposed to attacking big broad monster issues. While they are still measuring performance, posting results on public dashboards and trying to connect performance information to budgeting, the increase in evidence-based information, more data sharing, and greater sophistication in data analysis, has helped performance managers to generate results on individual topics where they see the potential for genuine improvement.

"For us, it has been a shift from focusing on the data to focusing on the problems," says James Wagner, chief of performance and innovation in Tulsa, Oklahoma. "That's the fundamental shift to us. What is the problem we're trying to solve?"

With each additional new approach, new lessons are learned. "I think all of this is better than it has ever been," says Funkhouser. "The work today is so much more sophisticated than thirty years ago. Performance management is more realistic and human centered and compassionate than it was. It is much less mechanistic."

Box 4.2 | Five Major Changes over the Last Thirty Years

The performance management field has consistently been plagued by a variety of pitfalls that will be discussed in this book. It is often underresourced, plagued by the indifference or outright resistance of political leaders, has problems of sustainability, and has trouble living up to expectations. Here are some of the most significant changes we've seen in the way that state and local governments build performance systems to deal with these issues:

1. Performance management efforts are now more frequently housed in separate clearly identified performance offices, less frequently regarded as an add-on responsibility for budget or planning departments.

2. More governments are appointing individuals to specific roles within the performance management field. Chief data officers, chief performance officers, chief innovation officers, and chief operating officers are proliferating and at least sometimes are seated at the right hand of the mayor, city manager, county administrator, or governor.

3. Attention has shifted from performance reporting to using performance information to solve problems.

4. Cross-department collaboration and departmental data sharing are increasingly used to address issues that inevitably spread over many different siloed programs and agencies.

5. Performance measurement is not a stand-alone function but part of a suite of performance initiatives that include strategic planning, data analysis, process improvement, and evaluation.

CASE STUDY

Service Efforts and Accomplishments

In June 2010, the Governmental Accounting Standards Board released a document titled "Suggested Guidelines for Voluntary Reporting of Performance Information."[19]

The GASB used yet another kind of wording for this effort, referring not to performance management but rather to "Service Efforts and Accomplishments." The project involved nearly twenty years of work to establish a recommended framework for providing citizens with performance information to supplement and add to their understanding of financial accounting and reporting information, the fields that were generally the GASB's province.

The guidelines themselves weren't problematic. But the GASB's entire foray into this field became the subject of controversy. As *Governing* publisher Mark Funkhouser observed in a *Governing* magazine column in 2013, the bitter debates regarding GASB over service efforts and accomplishments (SEA) reporting "reached a level of vitriol that would astonish those who imagine auditors and accountants to be introverted, passionless bean-counters."

The fierce debate over SEA took place over the course of the two decades that GASB was working on the project. Its primary main opponent was the Government Finance Officers Association (GFOA), an organization that seeks to advance excellence in state and local government financial management and has about twenty thousand members who work in public finance fields across the United States and Canada.

In 1993, GFOA argued in an adopted policy statement that involvement in state and localities reporting of outcome indicators "would exceed both the GASB's jurisdiction and its technical competence." As far as GFOA was concerned, the GASB should be sticking to its core competencies in accounting and public sector financial reporting.[20]

The GASB's response to objections that were repeated through the years that followed was that the guidelines it intended to develop for reporting performance measures were intended to be voluntary, used only by governments that elected to use them.

GFOA was not mollified. In another adopted policy statement in 2002, its objections were even more fiercely stated. Noting that it opposed the effort in "the strongest possible terms," it wrote:

> Even were GASB to establish completely "voluntary" measures of performance for those governments that wish to use them, the very existence of benchmarks established by a national standard-setting body would put pressure on governments to conform their own performance measures to GASB's model measures.[21]

By the early 2000s, multiple other organizations had joined GFOA in opposing the GASB's work in this area. While the Association of Government Accountants and the National Center for Civic Innovations were supportive of the SEA concept, multiple other state and local organizations joined GFOA in opposing it. These included the National Governors Association (NGA), the National Association of State Budget Officers (NASBO), the Council of State Governments (CSG), the International City/County Management Association (ICMA), the National Association of Counties (NACO), and six other public sector management organizations. Together they formed the National Performance Management Advisory Committee, which issued its final report, *A Performance Management Framework for State and Local Government*, in June 2010.

Following the almost simultaneous release of the GASB's suggested SEA reporting guidelines and the Performance Management Framework report, attention to SEA reporting gradually dwindled. Although a number of local governments paid heed to the guidelines in their own annual reports, all but a handful stopped using the GASB SEA terminology.

Despite the controversy, the substantial explorations that went into SEA reporting yielded guidelines for communicating performance information that are still very useful. Here is an edited and shortened version of the sixteen key recommendations that were provided in a 2003 report that included "Suggested Criteria for Effective Communication."[22]

GASB's Guidelines for Reporting Performance Information, 2003:

1. Clearly state the purpose and scope of the report.
2. Clearly state the major goals and objectives of the organization.
3. Include a discussion of the involvement of citizens, elected officials, management, and employees in establishing goals and objectives.
4. Present performance information at different levels or layers of reporting so users can find the level of detail they need.
5. Include executive or management analysis that objectively discusses results for the reporting period.
6. Focus on key measures that provide the basis for assessing results for major critical programs and services.
7. Provide information that will help readers assess the reliability and credibility of reported performance measures.
8. Use performance measures that are relevant and linked to mission, goals, and objectives.
9. Provide information about resources and costs and relate cost to outputs or outcomes.
10. Include citizen and customer perception of quality and results of services, when applicable.
11. Provide comparative information to help assess performance (e.g., to past periods or peer entities).
12. Include discussion of external and internal factors that may have a significant effect on performance.
13. Provide both aggregated and disaggregated information.
14. Be consistent from period to period of what is measured (and when a change is necessary make note of it).
15. Communicate through channels appropriate to the organization and its intended users.
16. Report on a regular basis and as soon after the reporting period as possible.

5

Outcomes

■ ■ ■

BACK IN THE 1990S, discussions about performance measurement often focused on the topic of inputs, outputs, and outcomes. It was important to know the following:

- Inputs—The resources put into an activity, like the total operating budget to run a particular state prison for a year.
- Outputs—A numerical measure of the goods or services purchased with the inputs such as new monitoring devices posted among inmates to detect early signs of a dangerous situation.
- Outcomes—The actual results of the activity, which in the prison example could be the impact of the outputs on reducing inmate violence.

The focus on terminology, at the time, made sense because many governments that were measuring performance still had a counting-oriented focus that put less attention on the real-world results of the outputs being purchased. Cities could tell you how many tons of garbage were collected, but not how clean the streets were. They could tote up the number of job training sessions that were held, but not how many individuals who were trained ended up with good jobs.

Nascent efforts at performance measurement in Little Rock, Arkansas, were typical of governments that were just moving forward toward using performance management to discern the value to the citizenry of their programs. Back in the 1990s and early 2000s, each Little Rock division had to report on revenues, expenditures, and "little infinitesimal details" about programs and participants, according to Melissa Bridges, performance and innovation chief. "It was 'Let's report a number to report a number so we can say we're doing our job.' "

In those days, the effort was often left to the budget office, which sent a form to departments on an annual basis so that they could gather and fill out numbers that represented their work for the previous year, the current year, and an estimate of the upcoming one. For example, Animal Control reported how many dog licenses it had handed out. As Bridges says, "To me, it wasn't necessarily meaningful. You'd have to have a number, just to report a number, because that's what you were asked to do. We weren't having a conversation about why there was an uptick in different problems. It was a regurgitation of numbers." In this case, it might be great to increase the number of dogs to which licenses had been recorded, but if the dogs weren't actually wearing them, no difference was made.

In the years that we evaluated governments first in *Financial World* and then in the Government Performance Project, we watched governments evolve in their understanding of the measures that could be most useful to them and what the data behind the measures could tell them.

Sharon Erickson, the recently retired longtime auditor of San Jose, remembers an important change that occurred in the way her city measured the cleaning of sewer pipes—and the lesson that it taught the city.

Back in the 1990s, the emphasis was on the number of pipes cleaned (an output measure). That led to a discovery by crews who were under pressure to clean more pipes. What's the easiest way to do that? "If they focused on cleaning cleaner pipes, their machines could get the job done more quickly," says Erickson.

Ultimately, that did nothing to stop sewer overflows, backups, or other problems that stem from clogged pipes.

By the early 2000s, the department changed the way it monitored progress from the number of pipes cleaned to measuring the reduction in sewer overflows. That led to a shift in focus from cleaning more pipes to predicting and dealing with pipes that were in danger of causing problems.

The new objective meant exploring key questions about where overflows were occurring, what caused problems to occur, and whether different problems required different fixes. One discovery: the biggest problems were not occurring in the major pipes but in the smaller ones, which were more likely to get clogged.

For San Jose, clarity on the objective—fewer sewer overflows—led to success in reducing the unpleasant implications of sludge pouring into the streets (see figure 5.1). It also contributed to increased insight about how to most effectively direct resources.

As performance measurement has evolved, far more questions are being asked about the measures and the data underlying them. "Now

Figure 5.1 Sewer Stoppages and Overflows Cleared

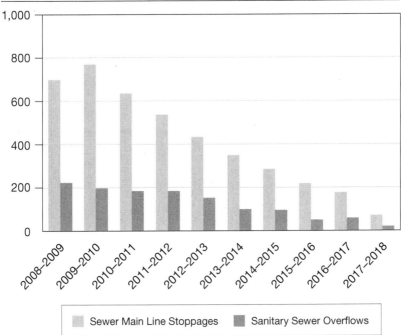

With a shift of focus to measuring results, San Jose has continued to reduce sewer overflow problems.
Office of the City Auditor, San Jose

we're getting better at understanding what the information is telling us," says Bridges. We're getting better at asking questions of the data and the questions we're asking are changing."

KNOWING THE GOAL

Performance measurements help governments assess their progress at reaching big-picture results—clean streets, a reduction in traffic fatalities, or an increase in adult literacy. "We're all seeking the best possible outcomes for residents in the most cost-effective way," says Maia Jachimowicz, vice president for evidence-based policy implementation at Results for America.

Some results are harder to measure than others. State transportation departments have strong results measures for determining the safety of their roads, but measuring congestion is more complex. Turnover in jobs is easy to measure, but the quality of the workforce is much harder to determine. Many administrative functions, like the quality of a mayor's work, can be nearly impossible to identify and quantify.

In general, states have a harder time making progress on results measures than cities. At the city level, managers can easily see the effects of most of the services they deliver and can also attach measures to the priorities voiced by their citizens. Are the streets clean? Is the trash picked up on time? Has crime dropped? Do buses keep to a schedule upon which commuters rely? These are precisely the kinds of things that matter to residents. Counting up the number of police on the streets as many cities do, is nearly irrelevant to citizens unless they contribute to less crime and a greater sense of safety.

Big broad results can be particularly difficult to measure. Efforts to reduce poverty or lead to cleaner air and water involve multiple agencies tackling challenging social problems that encompass large diverse populations over broad geographic areas. As a result, it can be difficult to chart progress and a frustrating task to achieve impact, particularly over a short time frame.

"That's why cities have become the power users of this stuff. They can take actions and see month-to-month, quarter-to-quarter change," says Ken Miller, author of several books about government performance and the founder of the Change and Innovation agency, which works with state human service agencies "to increase their capacity to do more good."[1]

Working on the staff of Missouri governor Mel Carnahan in the late 1990s, Miller saw that though the governor retained his enthusiasm, it was hard for everyone to stay engaged when the impacts of new strategies on outcome measures would likely not appear for years. "Some of these measures may not change in the course of an administration," says Miller.[2]

Big picture efforts to make the link between government performance measures and broader community results have skidded to a halt in Florida, Minnesota, and, most recently, Virginia, where the Council on Virginia's Future created and displayed the Virginia Performs dashboard, which looked at how the government and its measures affected quality of life for Virginia residents. The Council was sunset on July 1, 2017.

One of the best-known efforts to connect agency measures to larger community results was attempted in Oregon, with the Oregon Benchmarks and Progress Board, which bit the dust in 2010. (See box 5.1: The Demise of Oregon Benchmarks.)

What's more, the kinds of programs run by states often depend on multiple other players including counties and nonprofit that deliver services that states and the federal government fund. Just as states often dictate to counties what they should be measuring, the federal government requires that states provide a wide variety of performance measures that they would not necessarily choose for themselves.

For example, in the Temporary Assistance for Needy Families program (TANF), the federal government asks states to collect a "work participation rate" for benefit recipients. The federal government provides states with twelve ways in which a person receiving benefits can be added to the list of those that fulfill this requirement.

They can participate in community service programs or on-the-job training, but only a small number of the items on the list of "federally qualified activities" have to do with having a job.[3] Some states, like Colorado, have developed their own ways of tracking actual work

Box 5.1 | The Demise of Oregon Benchmarks

Over the years, states have launched a variety of efforts to try to connect the strategies and results measures of their agencies to larger community results. The most ambitious of these efforts was known as Oregon Benchmarks, launched in 1989 to track progress on the state's strategic plan. That same year, the Oregon Progress Board was established to oversee the effort. The goal was to provide a real-world context for citizens as well as to guide agencies toward creating their own performance measures.

The Oregon Progress Board lasted twenty rocky years. The number of benchmarks fluctuated, at one point reaching as high as 300 (at which point it was joked that the city had benchmarks on its benches). The number then settled to a more manageable 92. Every other year, the Oregon Progress Board would report on progress, but doubts surfaced along the way as to how much this consistent eye on outcome trends led to performance improvement efforts.[a]

In the first decade of the twenty-first century, the Progress Board continued to run short of funding. Recessions not only ate into state funds but also the blows they dealt to societal progress led to disillusionment about the difficulty in really affecting change.

The board never connected well with the legislature, with individual legislators complaining about the number of measures and the lack of concrete accomplishments associated with the effort. Some legislators felt that "unachievable targets" made them "vulnerable to constituent criticism when unrealistic goals were not met," according to then executive director Jeff Tryens.[b] Skeptics speculated that legislators were simply fearful that failures would be exposed, to their detriment on Election Day.

The program was ultimately permanently defunded and the Oregon Progress Board was wiped out of existence in 2010. (This did not stop the state's performance measurement efforts. In the "2018 Invest in What Works State Standards of Excellence," published by Results for America, Oregon was still listed as one of the leading states in having a data-driven and evidence-based approach.[c])

[a]Jeffrey Tryens, "Using Indicators to Engage Citizens: The Oregon Progress Board Experience," OECD World Forum on Key Indicators," November 13, 2004, 6.
[b]Tryens, 4.
[c]Results for America, *2018 Invest in What Works State Standards of Excellence*, July 10, 2018, 3, https://results4america.org/tools/state-standard-of-excellence-2018-invest-in-what-works-state-standard-of-excellence/.

participation (following data about whether or not individuals have entered employment) but the majority make do with what the federal government requires, whether or not it fulfills their ability to affect actual employment.

Tracking progress toward the big results desired by mayors and governors is obviously important, but often the core utility of performance measures is connected to interim objectives that lead to the big accomplishments. Research has long drawn a connection between the use of seatbelts and a decline in automobile fatalities; cutting down on teenage drinking may be an interim indicator that can lead to a decline in teenage pregnancy or sexually transmitted diseases; police programs that pay when unregistered guns are voluntarily handed in may reduce crime rates.

While performance measures are often intended to improve outcomes, a variety of information is needed to understand how those results can be achieved. "You can have measures that tell how efficient you are and some workload measures for context. You need a palette of measures that paints a picture of the outcome you're trying to achieve," says Brent Stockwell, assistant city manager in Scottsdale, Arizona.

STRIVING FOR EFFICIENCY

When Mayor Ben Walsh took office, in Syracuse, New York, in January 2018, he inaugurated an Office of Performance, Accountability and Innovation as one of his first administrative moves.

The mayor's ultimate vision for Syracuse involved economic growth, attention to diversity, and increased opportunity. But in order to accomplish lofty goals, he believed the city, which had ongoing budget troubles, had to operate more effectively than in the past. In the first year of his term, the performance team focused on objectives and performance measures—key results in their terminology—that they had some control over and could be measured effectively.

Take potholes. Prior to the mayor's new approach, the city measured the number of potholes it filled with an avowed effort to fill ten thousand potholes annually. But this target, "picked out of a hat," in the words of Sam Edelstein, the city's chief data officer, did not consider how many potholes were in need of filling.

Syracuse might have considered measuring the smooth ride residents experienced on city streets, but that takes time and money. For the moment, its more modest goal sufficed. The Department of Public Works has determined that a pothole should be filled within five days of the complaint coming in. Other departments have established their own optimal timelines for the delivery of service. Collectively, Syracuse is aiming to get 95 percent of work accomplished in the "established resolution time" for different functions.

As of April 2019, the city wasn't entirely successful but had met its time targets 76 percent of the time. Pothole filling was running a bit behind that at 57 percent. Notwithstanding actual rates of success, however, the capacity to see whether they were improving or not has been critical to helping to allocate resources.

Furthermore, measurements themselves are only one part of the performance management system. Each Wednesday, all Syracuse department heads come together with the mayor to discuss the city's progress. The first half-hour of these meetings always centers around one of the city's four objectives and one of the three key results attached to it. The objectives:[4]

- Achieve fiscal sustainability
- Increase economic investment and neighborhood stability
- Provide quality constituent engagement and response
- Deliver city services effectively, efficiently, and equitably

The emphasis is not just in having a measure but in studying it and thinking about what the data is communicating. One important consideration for time-related efficiency measures, for example, is the potential unintended consequences of moving too fast.

SELECTING TOP-LEVEL MEASURES

There's an old joke about a man named Ben who comes across a friend searching up and down a street for a lost watch. The man inquires, "Where did you lose the watch?" The answer, "Two blocks to the left." Ben: "Then why are you looking here?" And the final response: "The light is better."

This old tale is an allegory for governments that decide what to measure based on readily available data—the elements of government that are easy to measure rather than what may be more important.

Marc Holzer is the executive director of the National Center for Public Performance at Suffolk University in Boston.[5] The National Center has convened annual conferences on performance measurement and improvement since 1974 and offers an online Certificate in Strategic Public Performance which awards certification to several dozen practitioners each year.

He says one ongoing difficulty that governments have is that they pick their performance measures without sufficient thought, based on the data that's available. "I think people are measuring what they can easily measure," he says. "I'm skeptical as to whether they're measuring what really matters to citizens. They're not involving stakeholders in the process enough and I don't think they're being particularly creative in terms of what the impact should be—what we need to do to solve enduring public problems."

Another common complaint is that sometimes governments measure indiscriminately, collecting information on hundreds of indicators that confuse managers and overwhelm decision makers. In the mid-1970s, New York City was a pioneer in performance measurement, starting its *Mayor's Management Report* to collect and disseminate its many measures in one place.

But it tried to measure so much that by the early 1990s, the report was about the size of a pre-digital-age phone book. In the decade that followed, a still greater overabundance of data was nearly inevitable given the growth of the Internet and improving software. Online reports provided a virtually infinite amount of space available for more measures and the technological capacity to create them. But absorbing all that information was like trying to cross the Atlantic in a paddle boat.

Scottsdale's Brent Stockwell was given the task of revitalizing the city's process and performance improvement efforts in 2009. He started looking at the city's performance measures. There were 650 of them.

He printed out multiple pages of measures and taped them together. In a meeting with the city manager, he sat at one end of a long table, with the city manager at the other end. To start the meeting, he rolled out his long list from end to end on the table's surface (see photo 5.1), then asked the city manager to look at his list and decide how well Scottsdale was doing generally.

The answer: "Brent, I can't." No surprise there. Data, by itself, is meaningless without analysis. And clear-headed analysis is nearly impossible when there's more information than the human mind can assimilate.

To deal with an overload of measures, Scottsdale provided training and coaching sessions to managers on making choices of what performance measures to focus on and what data was really needed. "We tried to be sure that what they were measuring was consistent with their mission, and that they focused on the critical few not the abundant many. You need to help people understand what to look at as a manager to understand your services and how you're operating."

Too Much of a Good Thing.
Scottdale's Brent Stockwell unravels his very long list of performance measures.
City of Scottsdale

Of course, different kinds of measures are more or less useful depending on individual roles. In a new approach undertaken by Austin, the city's performance team is giving more thought to what is being measured, how it will aid in management, and what audiences need different kinds of measurements.

Tier one measures are connected to the city's three- to five-year strategic plan, which was passed by the City Council in 2018 with a great deal of stakeholder involvement (see chapter 6). These are the limited big outcomes that the city is aiming for over an achievable time period.

Tier two are the "meat and potatoes" measurements for the departments—following the key deliverables that fall under the department's mission.

Tier three is then left up to the departments—what they have chosen to measure to solve the problems that they confront. The choice of measures inevitably changes over time, sometimes from year to year.

This all entails focus up-front on getting the right measures in place on which to focus, figuring out the data that's needed to track those measures, and making sure that different kinds of measures are directed at the audience that can best use them.

CITIZEN SURVEYS

There are some services delivered by state or local governments for which the best measure comes from citizen input. Some years ago, Portland, Oregon, altered its measurements of crime to include citizens' sensation of safety and the parts of the city in which they found it. One result was the discovery that people felt safer where there was more light. When they felt safer, in turn, they were more likely to be on the streets. And the more people on the streets, the less crime.

The ability to get responses to citizen surveys is growing, as online surveys become increasingly popular. Brooks Rainwater, senior executive and director of the Center for City Solutions at the National League of Cities told us, "a growing number of localities are going online to get answers from their constituents . . . over the last five years, there's been a rapid increase in the number of our cities using online surveys."

The capacity of these surveys is also growing with new technology. For example, a new company, POLCO, founded by Nick Mastronadi, who previously worked on a data science team at Amazon, is now working with cities to help them to reach out to the many residents who don't come to council meetings or minimally attended hearings.

The company's skills allow it to cross-reference citizen response, usually gathered through the Internet, and broken out by age, gender, and voting districts. The ability to generate responses in real time gives it the ability to gather material about issues as they occur—for example, seeking information about snow removal success in different parts of a city. Duplicate responses from the same individual, a hazard in Internet polling, are easily weeded out.

CONNECTING TO NATIONAL MEASURES

While state government managers may complain about the measurement dictates of the federal government, they also can take advantage of the benchmarking opportunities provided through federal goal setting and performance measurement.

One example is the long-standing effort in the federal government to define and track national health objectives, the thirty-year-old Healthy People initiative, with the most recent version, Healthy People 2020, launched in 2010.[6]

Among the many ten-year goals and measures tracked:[7]

- The reduction of unwanted pregnancies
- The incidence in the adult population of high blood pressure
- The reduction of infant deaths
- Children receiving recommended immunizations
- The percent of children, adolescents, and adults who visited the dentist in the last year
- The percentage of people who smoke

These national goals can be useful to states and local governments in setting out their own objectives. Data that show progress—or lack of progress—from one year to the next provide valuable historical perspective for the nation as a whole and a way for governments and community groups to measure state and local progress against a national benchmark.

CASE STUDY

Washington: Cross-Agency Collaboration

Few states have worked as long, hard, and consistently as Washington at developing systems to achieve better government results. The state's governors, from Gary Locke (1997 to 2005), to Christine Gregoire (2005 to 2013), and now to Jay Inslee (whose first term began in 2013), have embraced performance management, with a variety of different approaches to improve state outcomes.

The state's methods for measuring and achieving better outcomes have garnered national praise. But that does not mean that state leaders have felt that any iteration achieved perfection. As a result, there have been multiple efforts to learn from and build on the past.

Governor Locke's Price of Government initiative, for example, focused on a radically different approach to budgeting. Governor Gregoire's Government Management and Accountability Performance (GMAP) system centered on individual agencies, with high-level meetings held regularly to analyze agency results.

Results Washington, initiated through an executive order in 2013, oversees all the state's performance management endeavors, which include Lean continuous improvement efforts, active outcome-oriented performance measurement, result reviews by the governor, and performance reporting through a public-facing dashboard.[8]

One of the biggest lessons that can be learned by other states as well as counties and cities from Washington: cross-agency collaboration is an often-missed but critical route to success in performance management. This is an area of concentration in which Washington has made several advances and currently excels.

One endeavor, which ran from 2014 to early 2018, established "goal councils" (each made up of twelve to fifteen agency directors). The central Results Washington staff held six meetings a month, one with each of the goal councils and the sixth a "Results Review" with Governor Inslee. The councils were formed around five different goal areas: world-class education, prosperous economy, sustainable energy and a clean environment, healthy and safe communities, and efficient, effective, and accountable government.

In the words of a Harvard case study, the job of the councils "was to set performance targets, and then to come up with strategies to achieve their goal and to devise ways to measure progress towards targets":

> The results review includes all leaders responsible for delivering on that goal. For example, if the discussion is about reducing traffic fatalities, then the related issues of drinking, drug use, speeding, driver age, and distracted driving will all be discussed. As a result, voices at the table will include the Washington State Patrol, the state Traffic Safety Commission, the Department of Licensing, the Department of Health, the Superintendent of Public Instruction, the Department of Social and Health Services, the Department of Corrections, the Department of Transportation, and Washington's Liquor and Cannabis Board.[9]

As of the end of 2017, Results Washington was tracking 190 different objectives through its interagency teams. At the time 52 percent were on track to meet targets and 41 percent were not. Seven percent were at an early stage of development.

In many ways the goal council system was successful at promoting cross-agency collaboration and coordinated performance improvement, but it still ran into multiple challenges, which culminated in the state's moving on to another approach.

One problem that Results Washington experienced—an issue common to many performance management systems—was that the goal council work was overwhelming. The meetings for department directors were time-consuming, particularly as subgoals and subgoal councils emerged from the larger groups.

Another issue was that even the effort to solve the problem of siloed agency activity created its own "shadowed silo system," says Inger Brinck, director of Results Washington. Setting up separate goal councils acted as an unexpected barrier to a more comprehensive view of problems. "There weren't conversations across the sectors," says Brinck.

To some extent, the councils also isolated performance management discussions from other players. "Performance measurement and continuous improvement isn't an add-on or side project, it needs to be integrated into government," says Hollie Jensen, director of Continuous Improvement, Results Washington.

Figure 5.2 Results Washinton Integrated Performance Management and Continuous Improvement System

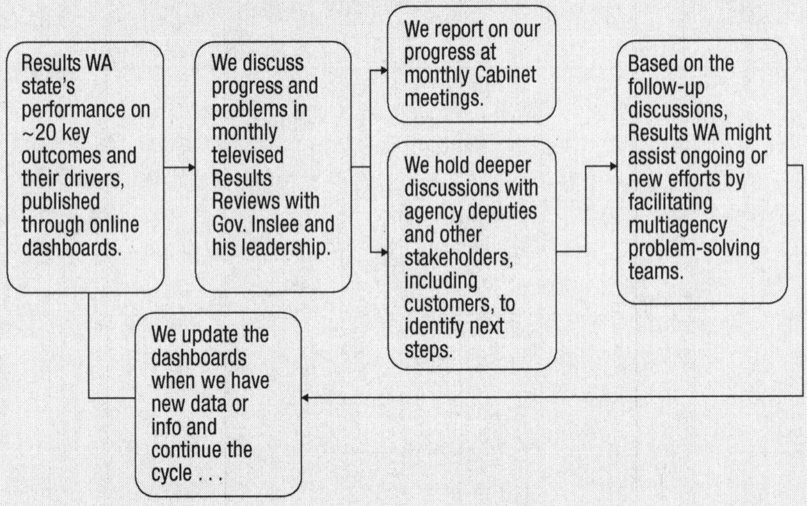

The path to Washington's multiagency problem-solving. Results Washington's Mission: To create a more responsive, data-driven, and human-centered state government.
Results Washington

To fix the problems of the goal council—a laudable effort despite its shortcomings—the state built upon its work to take another step forward.

For example, the state's 190 objectives were too many for the central Results Washington team to address, particularly since many were single agency objectives that did not need the collaborative focus of Results Washington. Instead, the central Results team is now focusing on twenty key priorities held by the governor or by state agencies. The rest of the objectives are left to the agencies themselves.

The new focus on a limited set of outcomes frees up the Results Washington team to do much of the data work and analysis itself rather than depending on departments to do it (see figure 5.2). This means it takes deeper dives into the data, doing much more analysis of geospatial and racial variation in the way services are delivered. It also allows the team to focus more on solutions to problems that emerge, incorporating a wide variety of performance management approaches, and involving multiple agencies, to achieve the governor's objectives.

As of April 2019, there were fifteen active outcome measures listed on the Results Washington website and six more in development. By reducing the number of outcome measures, managers were able to track pivotal information on the drivers that lead to results—"the factors that make a difference in whether an outcome is achieved," says Brinck.

One of the fifteen outcomes is "Supporting Successful Reentry"—a primary focus for Governor Inslee, who signed an executive order in 2016 to build up support for former inmates to readjust to community life.[10] Narrative text attached to the outcome measure explains that seven thousand individuals are released from Washington's adult correctional facilities each year and the state's objective is to reduce the three-year rate of recidivism, which reached its peak in 2003 at close to 35 percent, with the last three-year rate count in 2013 at 31.4 percent.[11]

In many governments, that objective would be considered the responsibility of the Department of Corrections. But Washington is coordinating "collaborative results teams," which are flexible enough to deal with individual issues of concern. Under the auspices of such a team, there are at least eight agencies involved in pushing for successful reentry.

In addition to the Department of Corrections, the participating agencies are involved with topics that are considered drivers for successful reentry, based on substantial past research and evaluation: housing, health care, social connections, education and training, and employment. So, for example, the strategy to increase the employment of recently released inmates includes the Department of Licensing and the Department of Commerce.

The state's analysis shows that employment success is aided by assuring reentry plans are launched before men and women have left prison. This has led to apprenticeship training and certification efforts for different jobs that require licensing. That gave managers the complex task of safely providing Internet access in prison. "A lot of certifications provide online tests. Now with internet access we can open up those jobs," says Crista Johnson, senior performance advisor for Results Washington.

Between 2010 and 2018, the postrelease employment rate has gone up from 26 percent to 36.5 percent.

Megan Macvie, former Results Washington communication advisor, worked for the state between 1999 and March 2019 and during that time saw multiple iterations of performance management. The current version, she says, has been successful at empowering the multiple diverse participants who are encouraged to contribute ideas. "The group helps to facilitate not only the conversation in the room, but the problem solving that comes after. People are energized and excited about bringing solutions to the governor."

6

Performance Budgeting

■ ■ ■

PERFORMANCE MANAGEMENT has had success in making positive changes in policy and management. Yet, for many, the conversation concentrates more on influencing city councils, county commissions, and state legislatures to use performance information to build budgets. This performance-based budgeting, as it is often called, encounters frequent challenges.

Philip Joyce is senior associate dean of the School of Public Policy at the University of Maryland. He and other experts indicate that while efforts have emerged to change the ethos of budgeting practices, they have often faced multiple political and practical obstacles. (See case study on Illinois on page 68.)

He favors talking about "performance-informed" budgeting as opposed to performance-based budgeting. This better communicates the idea that the information that is gathered in performance management efforts can and should be used by budgeters and other decision makers, including legislators. But it makes clear the fact that there is no actual formulaic connection among measures, evaluations, and budgets. Performance-informed budgeting is also the preferred term used by the executive director of the National Association of State Budget Officers, John Hicks.

But although it may be difficult to build performance information into the budget process, when the fiscal year is over, performance audits, management reviews, and evaluations can use performance information to assess the impact of spending decisions and help determine how objectives can be more effectively and efficiently achieved in the future.

PERFORMANCE BUDGETING LEGISLATION

The question of how many states practice performance budgeting is complex, according to a 2015 NASBO "spotlight" on how states use performance data in budgeting. This question "may sound straightforward," but "coming up with the answer can be tricky," it reported.

"Whether states use a performance-based approach to budgeting is not typically a straightforward 'yes' or 'no' answer; in fact, performance budgeting use at the state level should probably be viewed along a continuum from minimal to extensive use, with significant variation on how this is accomplished."[1]

Whether the states use performance information in their budgeting, most have legislation that intends to link their budgeting process with measures of performance in some way. The most recent count, reported by Elaine Yi Lu and Katherine Willoughby in their 2018 book, *Public Performance Budgeting: Principles and Practice*, is that forty-two states currently have some kind of performance budgeting in statute.[2]

As Lu and Willoughby write, the lack of a performance budgeting law "does not preclude use of performance budgeting." At the same time, the existence of a law does not "necessarily lead to strong practices."[3]

In the 1970s, Hawaii was one of the pioneers of performance budgeting. But by the 1990s, the requirements for producing outputs and outcomes in the budget had faded into disuse with only a few departments consistently delivering effective information to the budget office. The performance budgeting statute had been ignored for so long, that legislators in 1998 established a task force to examine the possibility of performance-based budgeting. As one official told us with a sigh, "we had to testify to them that we already had it."

IMPEDIMENTS

A major issue that can preclude the use of performance in the appropriation process is the large number of players who are often involved and represent constituencies with a wide variety of needs. This can lead to decision makers thinking more about partisan loyalty and the next election than about good management. Few can win popular support based on the application of performance measures, data analysis, or program evidence to their decisions. When was the last time you saw a lawn sign with the wording, "Smith for Mayor: Better Measurement Today"?

"We hear about budget officers or analysts being uncertain of how much the information is really being used by legislatures in actually making budgetary decisions," says Hicks. "If either the executive or legislative branch of government doesn't act, use, or thoughtfully consider this information, then the energy wanes."

Frustration stems from disappointment when the benefits touted by advocates fail to materialize. Logically, information on performance should help during an economic downturn in making strategic reductions, avoiding blunt actions that can sometimes cost a government money rather than saving money. Consider the cut to tax departments that reduce the number of auditors who are generating additional revenues based on their analyses. A ProPublica investigation notes that the IRS has cut the number of its auditors by a third since 2010, and estimates that these cutbacks create a "toll of at least $18 billion every year."[4]

A 2011 study at the University of Georgia looked back at the impact of performance budgeting on the 2007–2009 recession and previous ones. It found little sign that performance information was used in making cuts. The study, published in *Public Administration Review*, found some evidence that performance data were used in good times, but not during downturns. An excerpt:

> Program cost and service reductions are too numerous and significant to be "intelligent": personnel changes, such as furloughs, early retirements, salary reductions, and layoffs seem to be more desperate than "smart". Services at the bare bones are kept regardless of performance.[5]

A performance audit of Louisiana in 2012 surveyed agencies and found that more than half did not think legislators paid attention to performance information when making budgeting decisions. Both executive and legislative interviewees complained about the lack of relevance of measures, difficulty in finding information, measurement inaccuracy, too much data, and a system that was not user-friendly.

Furthermore, in state government, substantial sections of the budget are on "auto-pilot." States need to take care of their debt service and liabilities; public school funding is based on formulas and the number of children enrolling; Medicaid eligibility rules dictate state Medicaid spending. These costs are often out of the hands of decision makers when budgets are debated.

This is particularly true at the federal level. In a paper delivered at the 2018 Association for Public Policy and Management (APPAM) conference, Phil Joyce summed up the problem this way:

> You have to keep in mind 70 percent of the federal budget is on autopilot and there's no way that performance information is feeding into that 70 percent of the budget. Then the other 30 percent is half defense and half non-defense. So, a lot of the decisions that do rely on performance are at the margins. When the Obama administration used performance information to target programs for elimination in the federal budget during the Great Recession, the proposals amounted to under 1 percent of federal spending.[6]

There are also technical issues that can derail potentially good systems, as can common management problems: a lack of capacity, weak communication, unmanageable quantities of information, and poor timing.

We have seen efforts to connect funding to performance fail even when there's a push to do so in one branch of government or one department. In Rhode Island, we observed back in the 1990s and early 2000s that the planning office was gung-ho about moving to more aggressive use of strategic planning and performance measurement, but the budget office was a separate entity that had minimal interest. Without the budget office to seamlessly provide data, the effort to measure and manage performance often flounders.

One problem that North Carolina ran into years ago was that the executive branch decided to organize its performance information in ten policy areas. Its focus on cross-agency goals put it ahead of other states, but the legislature was highly resistant to the organizational framework that the governor's office had established. One of the key problems was that the ten goal areas did not fit well with the legislature committee structure, which was organized differently.[7] This is precisely the kind of unintentional, structural barrier that can stymie government progress at all levels, not just in the realm of performance management.

Establishing and implementing performance funding systems can take many months or years. But impatience can derail these systems before they've had a chance to show their value.

In 2016, one of our *Governing* columns focused on the difficulty that states were having with performance funding for higher education. At the time, at least twenty states were experimenting with tying a small portion of the budgets for their university systems to performance on key objectives like first-year student retention or successful degree achievement.

At the time, we talked with Charles Sallee, the deputy director of the New Mexico Legislative Finance Committee. He was concerned that his state's performance-based higher education funding was short on details and that the colleges and universities were cannibalizing each other in the fight for dollars. Too little attention was paid to the mission of different institutions and the individual challenges they faced.[8]

Three years later, we talked with Sallee again and his tone was far more positive. Some of the same challenges remained but the state had also begun to see results. "Frankly, the universities have responded pretty well," he told us in spring 2019.

A 2018 program evaluation noted that even a low level of performance funding appeared to have motivated some New Mexico institutions to make changes to increase the number of students who complete their degrees. For example, enhanced student advising was credited with a rise in the four-year graduation rate from the University of New Mexico from 16.7 percent in 2014 to 32.5 percent in 2018.

The performance funding system in New Mexico is by no means perfect as the evaluation makes clear. Looking at higher education in general in the state, much of the increased degree production has been in lower level certificates and associate's degrees. For example, the evaluation, which made a number of recommendations, counseled that incentives needed strengthening to produce more of an impact on at-risk students.[9]

ATTENTION TO EVIDENCE

The most dramatic performance budgeting development in recent years has been the targeted efforts to connect funding to programs that have tangible evidence of success.

Back in the 1990s, discussions of performance budgeting focused very closely on whether budget objectives were informed by performance measurements. Increasingly, executive and legislative branch members are being offered real-world stories of success by agencies hoping to persuade them that there is value to their work—and that it is worth paying for.

Recently, NASBO assembled an inventory of state initiatives that connect the use of program data and evidence to funding decisions. The organization's intent is to update the list on a regular basis. As of November 2018, there were ninety-one initiatives listed, falling into the following categories: data analytics, evidence-based policy-making, performance budgeting, performance management, and process improvement.[10]

A NASBO analysis points to multiple states adding funding to evidence-based programs for both fiscal years 2019 and 2020. For example, in Florida, the governor's 2020 budget proposal included $12.3 million for evidence-based programs for the Department of Juvenile Justice and in North Carolina, the governor's budget proposed roughly $3 million for evidence-based family preservation services.[11]

Proposals for increased funding based on evidence of past program or policy success have parallels in many other states and local governments, although it often involves very small portions of a budget. For example, although much of Colorado's fiscal year 2019 $30.5 billion executive budget was dictated by requirements in law, commitments to fund benefit programs, and major outlays for education and health, funding decisions for multiple small programs were based on agencies' capacity to provide real-world evidence that these were worthwhile investments.

About $625,000 in funding—representing a 100 percent hike—was allocated in the 2019 executive budget to expand an evidence-based mental health program to two thousand more children and families.[12] This was based on a cost-benefit analysis that found the program returned $4 for every $1 expended.[13]

BUDGET EXECUTION

The most negative assessments of the use of performance budgeting come from the work done at the central level: through legislatures, city councils, mayors, and governors. But one step down in the governmental food chain, agencies are far more likely to use performance information to influence the use of dollars over which they have control. This includes not just implementation of their annual or biannual budgets, but also the way they distribute federal and other grants.

Elke Shaw Tulloch, administrator of Idaho's Division of Public Health, explained the impact of performance data on grant distribution to the Results First team at Pew in 2017. "When we get a grant from CDC or another federal agency, we then have to decide how to distribute across districts," she said. "This performance data helps us to target those dollars more strategically."[14]

"I don't think it has been well recognized that agencies have flexibility in terms of their management and resources," says Joyce. "You can call that budget execution or management, but it involves them making decisions about resources and that's part of performance budgeting."

This isn't to say that agencies have carte blanche to spend discretionary funds in whatever way performance measures lead them. In some states, agencies are limited in the amount of money they can transfer from one division to another. Their hands may also be tied if the state imposes a strict limit on moving cash from one line item to another—equipment, for example, to personnel.

States vary in the amounts they can transfer, as NASBO spells out in detail in its comprehensive 2015 *Budget Processes in the States* report.[15] As of that year, in Vermont, the amount that could be shifted from one agency to another was limited to $50,000. In Nebraska, transfers between programs were only allowed if specifically authorized in the budget bill. In Rhode Island, shifts between programs required legislative approval.

Even within an individual state, practices can differ depending on the agency involved. In Oregon, some agencies may receive an appropriation that is not designated by program, giving the agency director considerable freedom to make decisions. For other Oregon entities, the appropriations may be made in a way that is much more specific.

Generally, based on states' self-reporting in 2015, in fifteen states, the budget office could transfer money between departments. In more than twice that many it could transfer money between programs or units within a department.[16]

That's the broad-brush painting of state flexibility, but there are many details as spelled out in three pages of footnotes that appear in NASBO's *Budget Processes in the States*.[17]

THE ENVIRONMENT MATTERS

Whatever path performance management takes, integrating it with funding decisions requires leadership guidance, cooperation, and support from multiple players and a budget infrastructure that is compatible with using performance information. "Leadership is really important in sustaining these kinds of efforts and advancing the practice," says NASBO's John Hicks.

While performance management systems can exist without performance budgeting, it is unlikely that the latter could achieve success without a performance management culture to support it.

Many moving governmental parts need to be synchronized for performance budgeting systems to work well.

In 2016, Ivor Beasley, a lead public sector specialist at the World Bank, and Don Moynihan,[18] now the McCourt chair at Georgetown University's McCourt School of Public Policy, studied efforts to link budgets to performance in Australia, Estonia, France, Netherlands,

Poland, Russia, and the United States. Writing in the Public Financial Management Blog in early 2017, they included recommendations of ways that performance budgeting can be strengthened.

Some of their key lessons, condensed and edited, are:

- Reduce complexity; select key goals and measures and avoid trying to deal with a "profusion of performance indicators" that can contribute to a "complex architecture of programs, subprograms and activities."
- Manage expectations and adjust the specific approach used to the administrative culture of the entity.
- Realize that operating a workable performance budgeting system takes time and money and the development of new skills.
- Consider "staged or partial approaches" to performance budgeting, if capacity is lacking.
- Recognize that performance budgeting does not just happen once a year during budget preparation and passage, but that review and discussion should occur throughout the year.
- Don't give up on a performance budgeting system because of problems; adapt as time progresses and difficulties appear. "Governments are too quick to abandon rather than adapt past efforts," Beasley and Moynihan write.

Beasley and Moynihan also say that performance budgeting "is more likely to succeed when it is part of a broad-based long-term government effort to introduce a more performance-oriented culture rather than being an isolated reform promoted by the central budget authority."[19]

For example, when Austin transformed its budget to match City Council objectives in 2018 (see case study), it benefited from strong leadership support, and a three-decade focus on government performance.

For two decades it has had a program budget, in which performance indicators are aligned with city programs. Moving to a new budgeting system that steered money to a limited number of strategically selected objectives was much easier than if the city's budgets had been produced based on line items or if using performance information was a newer concept.

CASE STUDY

Austin: A Budget with a Vision

In 2018, Austin transformed its budget process, moving from a system that focused on the city's three hundred individual programs to a budget aligned with the City Council's new strategic plan which had identified six areas of focus: economic opportunity and affordability; mobility; safety; health and environment; culture and lifelong learning; and "government that works for all"[20] (see figure 6.1).

This new approach made it easier for the council to comprehend the way in which programs worked with one another, and to detect duplication in appropriations requests more easily. It turned a morass of numbers into a comprehensible plan. This is an idea entirely in keeping with the general concept that a budget is, at heart, a sophisticated, number-laden plan leading to the future.

The twelve hundred performance measures that connected to the Fiscal 2018 budget were pared down to under two hundred strategic metrics that flowed from thirty-five major indicators, attached to

Figure 6.1 Austin Strategic Priority Setting

Economic Opportunity & Affordability
Housing
Homelessness
Skills and capability of our community workforce (including education)
Health & Environment
Accessibility to quality health care services, both physical and mental
Climate change and resilience
Accessibility to quality parks, trails, and recreational opportunities
Mobility
Accessibility to and equity of multimodal transportation choices
Safety
Fair administration of justice
Government that Works
Condition/quality of city facilities and infrastructure and effective adoption of technology
Culture & Lifelong Learning
Vibrancy and sustainability of creative industry ecosystem

City of Austin FY 2019 Approved Budget.

the six strategic objectives. This simplification stemmed from heavy lifting the council did in its year-long development of a strategic plan. One benefit of this flow of accomplishments was that for the Fiscal 2019 budget, the City Council deliberated for only six hours. The previous year's budget deliberations had taken three days.

In the six weeks that preceded the council's final deliberations, the usual mad rush of last-minute funding proposals—often numbering more than one hundred—just about disappeared.

The dramatically streamlined appropriation process won rave reviews from the city manager, the city's performance unit, community groups, and the City Council. Changing the budgeting approach was a lot of work, but the political and process improvements that emerged more than made up for the extra effort, says Ed Van Eenoo, the deputy chief financial officer who runs the budget office.

Hooking the budget to strategic objectives clarified the council's priorities and stopped it from passing random resolutions that might look appealing on a day-to-day basis, but could interfere with more pressing priorities, given the limitation of budget resources.

In the past, the budget office was often scurrying to see how it could find another $50,000 to fund a small initiative. Conversations about budget minutia distracted staff and politicians from thinking about the bigger picture.

"Without a council endorsed strategic plan, there was a lot of ad hoc budgetary decision making in previous budget cycles," Eenoo says. "Some of the resolutions they passed had serious cost implications. Without a broader context, it creates a problem. There isn't enough money to do everything."

How did the city manage to create such a beneficial strategic plan which tied budgetary decisions to outcomes?

The genesis was a thirteen-month initiative in which the eleven-member council tapped community stakeholders for their views, debated priorities, and established a comprehensive vision as to what they wanted to accomplish over the next three to five years.

In the Culture and Lifelong Learning area, for example, a narrative portion of the budget explains that multiple departments support the six priorities that fall under the topic:

- Literacy Advancement
- Workforce and Economic Development
- Digital Inclusion, STEM, and Computer Training
- Outreach and Community Engagement
- Equity, Diversity, and Inclusion
- Staff Development

Resources for these priorities are primarily divided among the Austin Public Library, the Economic Development Department, and the Parks and Recreation Department.

Narrative references in the approved fiscal 2019 Austin budget[21] are made to how the city is doing on some of its 150 plus metrics and citizen satisfaction information is spread throughout. For example, citizen satisfaction with library services is measured based on three separate categories: materials, quality, and cleanliness (see figure 6.2).

The rest of the metrics are available in the appendix to the new strategic plan.[22]

Of course, not all funding needs fall neatly into preset areas. Life just isn't that simple. "Operationalization is really important. There's a lot of tedious work," says Kimberly Olivares, Austin's chief performance officer. The city's budgeters had to look at departmental individual goals and key performance indicators to make sure they aligned with the city plan, but also make sure that other state or federal requirements weren't lost.

Figure 6.2 Citizen Satisfaction with Library Services

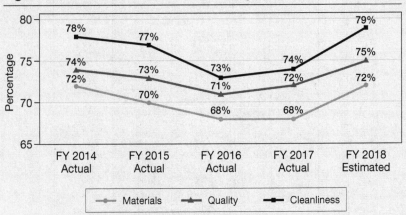

Trend lines help Austin keep tabs on residents' views of library services.
City of Austin FY 2019 Approved Budget.

Says Olivares, "What really gave us our success was that we didn't develop this plan behind closed doors." While organizing the new framework was carried out by city management, the City Council was always an active partner and significant attention was focused on tapping residents for input and then transforming the way budget information was delivered.

"We changed the way we communicate the budget externally based on the strategic outcomes," she says. "Instead of having to go department by department, we were suddenly able to talk about this in its totality."

CASE STUDY

Illinois: Unrealistic Expectations

Illinois is a good example of the daunting distance between "budgeting for results" dreams and reality.

In 2010, Illinois governor Pat Quinn signed a "Budgeting for Results" law, which was heralded as a way to stop the automatic funding of programs, and required the beleaguered state, with its pressing financial problems, to "live within its means and focus on performance," in the words of the first Illinois Budgeting for Results Commission annual report in November 2011.[23]

Eight years later, Jim Lewis, chair of the State of Illinois Budgeting for Results Commission, reflected on the state's experience to date.

"The initial legislation was overly ambitious. I don't think it can be implemented the way it was written," he says. "It called for the state to rank in order of efficiency all the programs the state operates and at the same time for the budget office to arrive at a revenue figure for the coming year and for the governor's budget to fund programs starting at the most efficient until it ran out of money.

"It couldn't happen like that."

In the first years after the legislation passed, the commission talked a lot, but didn't convert conversation into action. "In the Quinn administration, the commission conversations ranged very far and wide about state financial policy and budget process, and I'd say most of the recommendations dealing with broad based budgeting and economic conditions didn't appear to me to be fruitful," says Lewis. "I didn't see any game plan for implementation."

The commission continued to operate out of the limelight with little impact for about eight months after Bruce Rauner became governor in January 2015. In mid-summer of that year, seventeen of the twenty commissioners were not reappointed and nine more were appointed.

At that point, there was an effort at a restart, and the commission began working with the Illinois budget office to review 430 discrete programs, rewriting program objectives and searching for evaluation materials that would reveal each program's efficiency or effectiveness. It wasn't hard for commissioners to see that the budget office, with multiple other responsibilities, was not able to do the work itself, and initially the state sought technical assistance from the Pew Charitable Trusts-MacArthur Results First initiative to focus on the benefits and costs of a limited number of individual programs within the criminal justice field.

In July 2017, the Governor's Office of Management and Budget piloted this new approach in adult criminal justice. OMB began by comparing three current programs intended to reduce recidivism by individuals leaving state prison to a national research database to determine which programs were evidence-based and had been shown effective in addressing this key outcome. The analysis revealed that the three programs—correctional postsecondary education, correctional basic skills education, and vocational education in prison—were effective at reducing recidivism.

Based on these findings, recommendations were developed to further improve the programs by setting long-term goals, including targets and timelines, and expanding the use of these tools to other state policy priority areas such as health and education.

By the end of 2018, initial plans to build on this work in order to rank in order all the state's programs and budget according to efficiency were deferred indefinitely, in favor of a much more modest approach. The commission's December 2018 annual report showed the results of the analysis of the benefits and costs of seven programs within the Department of Corrections.[24]

This effort met with some success. But the idea that it can provide a launching pad to ultimately rank all the state's programs may take a lifetime to complete.

7

Pitfalls

■ ■ ■

MICHAEL JACOBSON IS deputy director for Performance and Strategy in King County's Office of Performance, Strategy and Budget. As mentioned in chapter 3, his county's efforts received the Center for Performance and Accountability Award for Organizational Excellence in February 2019.

That might lead his counterparts in other states to think that Jacobson and his colleagues had overcome most of the obstacles to performance management. But Jacobson's candid comments from August 2017 run to the contrary. At the time, he wrote the following in the Washington State–based Municipal Research and Services Center (MRSC) Insights blog: "Performance management is new, it's hard, it's not what people are used to, and it requires a different type of mental muscles, new thinking, and the adoption of new practices; all of which means change."[1]

Change, of course, is one of the most difficult tasks confronting governments that wish to be high-performing. Leaders in performance management encounter multiple pitfalls on the road to success. This chapter summarizes the ones that we've found to be most common.

INSUFFICIENT RESOURCES

Robin Rosenberg is a Socrata project manager at Tyler Tech, which acquired Socrata in 2018. "Our customers are very data-rich. They are also resource-poor," she says, citing a lack of people and the constant specter of government cuts. "The ability to solve the critical problems is hamstrung by the resources."

What's more, performance management systems are often started without an appreciation of the staff time it will take, particularly when performance tasks are tacked on to department responsibilities that may already be overwhelming.

The problem, of course, goes beyond having enough men and women on the payroll.

LACK OF DATA EXPERTISE

Too few employees know how to make the most out of the data collected. For example, geographic information systems (GIS) have increasingly been seen as a means for disaggregating data in a visually clear way that eases the route from raw data to understanding to action.

But a lack of expertise and training in universities across the country has been an obstacle. Many of the GIS courses are taught in schools of geography, an infrequently sought-out destination for college students. "We have to get information about GIS in front of our students," says Anthony G. Robinson, director for online geospatial education at Penn State University. "They're not coming in from high school with the idea that this is a work path."[2]

© iStock/Getty Images Plus/PeopleImages

WEAK INTERNAL TRAINING

Chapter 10 on data progress highlights the lack of skills in the workforce to take advantage of the easily available technical tools that can now be used to analyze and display information with the goal of improving services and government performance.

Beth Blauer, the executive director of the Centers for Civic Impact at Johns Hopkins University, says there needs to be a "doubling-down" in attention to the data skills of employees.[3] She is not talking about managers but about government employees at all levels who could benefit by knowing how to understand and use the data available to them in their jobs.

Even basic training of frontline staff in understanding the purpose—and potential—of the data that they're inputting could go a long way to improving basic problems of data quality.

Alarmingly, despite shortcomings, current government efforts to build employee performance management and data skills may now be at their all-time height. As soon as a recession hits, training opportunities slim down dramatically as do opportunities to travel to conferences or even to join professional associations that facilitate and promote knowledge sharing.

COUNTERPRODUCTIVE INCENTIVES

When incentives are used to reward employees, contractors, or programs for achieving desired objectives, they can change practices in negative ways.

One of the first stories that we heard when we started researching and reporting on government performance was about the Job Training Partnership Act. When local programs were rewarded for the number of economically disadvantaged trainees that they placed in jobs, some of them began to cherry-pick their trainees, signing on those who had a better chance of getting employed and turning away individuals whose prospects seemed dimmer.

That's an old story, but the issue has not gone away. Hanna Azemati, program director at Harvard University's Government Performance Lab, notes that performance incentives that tie dollars to placing job trainees in jobs may lead providers to prioritizing activities that favor immediate job placement rather than addressing a candidate's problems such as substance abuse that could interfere with sustainable employment. "Perhaps worse, the provider could feel pressure to serve clients who are the easier to place into jobs instead of those most in need of help," she writes in a 2018 *Governing* commentary.[4]

SLOW RESPONSE

Government is not known for its speed. It can take undue days, weeks, and months to build the launching pads necessary for solid performance management programs—and by the time the apparatus for making informed decisions has been established, the problem itself can easily have changed.

Hollie Jensen, director of continuous improvement with Results Washington, says one frustration for the individuals involved in Results Washington in Governor Jay Inslee's first term was that the meetings, which involved a great deal of departmental preparation and the involvement of cabinet officials, had to be planned well in advance. Result Washington's organizational structure at the time revolved around five goal councils with 192 measures that had been established to track those goals.

But staying current on emerging Washington issues was a challenge, Jensen says. In Governor Inslee's second term, the Results Team changed its approach, as we describe in chapter 5, but it is still a challenge to both deal with current initiatives and stay attuned to a new set of emerging problems.

LACK OF SUSTAINABILITY

A new administration can make many critical short-term gains but cannot count on its new systems being around over the long term. We talked with former Iowa governor Tom Vilsack just before he was named secretary of agriculture by President Obama. He was clearly disappointed by the way in which his successor as Iowa governor, a fellow Democrat, had dismantled his performance programs, which were working effectively.

In 2017, former Maryland governor Martin O'Malley told then *Governing* reporter J. B. Wogan about a conversation he had with Bill Bratton, the former New York City police commissioner who helped institute CompStat (see pages 87–89). As O'Malley recalled, "Bratton said to me, 'You know, Martin, the hardest things to institutionalize are new systems that require constant work.' . . . Just as easily, that rock will roll back down the hill if someone's not pushing it up."[5]

The now-you-see-it, now-you-don't world of performance management initiatives leads to the kind of employee resistance that we discuss in chapter 8. When there is an ethos of regular postelection upheaval, the men and women lower down in the ranks are disinclined to put their hearts and souls into any initiative. It's easier to just stick around and wait for a new effort to come and then ignore that one.

It's the "weebees," says Zachary Markovits, director of city progress at What Works Cities. "We be here before you got here, and we be here after you've gone."

THE PRACTITIONER–ACADEMIC DISCONNECT

Universities are extremely helpful to governments in analyzing data, evaluating programs, and researching program and policy impact. But over the years, we have heard many complaints about the lack of connection between the research agenda of academics and the practical needs of practitioners who are looking for academic assistance.

This is one of performance management expert Marc Holzer's favorite topics. He worries about formulaic academic research in which methodology is rewarded over substance. When there are important research findings, he believes that there is difficulty in communicating those messages to practitioners. He says, "I think what we need is more of a dialogue between the academics and the practitioners. Those who are publishing (research about) performance need to understand what things are like on the ground. That's a big problem. If you don't understand that. How can you develop a research agenda?"

FEAR OF ADVERSE REACTION

Benchmarking, in which practices that work can be borrowed from one local government to another or one state to another, can be extremely useful. But many benchmarking efforts have soured because of the fear that comes in exposing an entity to possibly damaging comparisons with peers.

In the 1990s, we were part of an advisory group that preceded the establishment of a comparative benchmarking program by the ICMA, the International City/County Management Association, known commonly just by its initials. We argued that it was critical that the findings be made public, but other advisory committee members argued that this would be an unworkable approach, because cities wouldn't want to be put in the politically difficult position of appearing to deliver inferior outcomes to those of their neighbors.

That mind-set has kept many governments from embarking on benchmarking efforts.

TOO MUCH HYPE

Few factors are more inclined to influence legislative behavior than disappointment. When a particular initiative in performance management fails to fulfill its promised benefits, opponents gain a great deal of power come the next legislative session.

Don Moynihan, McCourt Chair at the McCourt School of Public Policy at Georgetown University, recalls the "buyer's remorse" felt by some state and local government officials, who plunged into their own massive performance measurement systems following the introduction of the 1993 Government Performance and Results Act.

On the one hand, there was a systematic underestimate of the time and effort that come from aggressive and demanding performance management systems. But, on the other hand, there was also disappointment when new systems did not have a bigger or more immediate effect.

Unfortunately, a certain amount of hype is inevitable, regardless of its long-term risks. "It is easier to get a change in place if you promise that it is going to deliver people's highest hopes for government," says Moynihan. If instead, it's sold as an incremental tool that will help around the edges, "that's a less compelling argument."

FLAWS WITH TARGETS

Many performance management systems are based on setting and meeting targets. But, although targets have the benefit of encouraging and motivating employees and managers to strive to meet them, there are also potentially adverse consequences.

Potential pitfalls in targeting specific outputs or outcomes have become increasingly obvious to close observers. Jay Fountain is director of the Office of Policy and Management for Stamford, Connecticut, and for years spearheaded the Governmental Accounting Standards Board's work on performance reporting. "People establish targets and unfortunately, many don't understand why other than that they're being forced to," he says. "Then, they want to meet their targets, but they don't know what to do if they actually achieve or don't achieve them."

Let's say a city were to set a target that called for cutting response time for fire calls from six minutes to five minutes. If it reaches that target, does that mean the city should declare victory and move on to other issues? Or should it take this accomplishment as a sign that it can make life-saving progress and push further—even investing more resources—to do better still?

Says Alexandra Fercak, senior management auditor for Portland, Oregon's auditor's office, "Sometimes nobody can explain to you where the targets come from. And often people don't know what the targets are supposed to be used for."

Performance measurement and management expert Shelley Metzenbaum, who was associate director for Performance and Personnel Management at the Office of Management and Budget during the Obama administration, has a strong belief that an overemphasis on achieving targets is distracting and counterproductive.

"When governments emphasize the percentage of targets met, warning bells ought to be blaring," she says.

A LIMITED FOCUS

To keep from being overwhelmed by the information conveyed to them by multiple performance measures and a seemingly infinite supply of data, many performance managers have focused their efforts on using data to solve individual problems.

These efforts are highly worthwhile, but with too little time and resources, attention to a limited number of smaller problems may limit the ability of performance management to have wider impact.

The tendency to deal with smaller issues that can deliver results in a short time period is likely influenced by the often short tenure of elected officials who like to see that their initiatives are bringing about results during their administration—not ten years down the road.

But, as Holzer puts it, there's a valid concern that this approach doesn't make the big changes that will have noticeable impact on safety, health, or quality of life, but instead "focuses on the tiny stuff."

"You're saving pennies," he says. "What we need to do in the public sector is save lives and it's a whole different order of magnitude. You can keep doing incremental work but then you miss the big picture."

NEGLECT OF INTRACTABLE PROBLEMS

A focus on achieving outcomes may distract government leaders from confronting societal problems that are difficult to measure and have historically proven more difficult to solve.

Steven Rathgeb Smith, executive director of the American Political Science Association, says that an emphasis on measurement can push government agencies and foundations to direct more attention to easily measurable services. When outcomes are more uncertain—for example, among the chronically mentally ill—programs tend to get less focus and less funding, he says.

LEGISLATIVE INDIFFERENCE

When performance measurement and management efforts connect with budgeting or policymaking, as opposed to executive management functions, the reaction of legislators can be frustrating.

At the beginning of the Great Recession, the National Conference of State Legislatures looked at the use of performance information by legislators.[6]

It noted that numerous issues had been raised by both legislators and their staffs about the kinds of information they received, the kinds of indicators that were used, and the shortcomings in the way they were communicated. The complaints included the following:

- Indicators were not "well-chosen" and did not jibe with concerns of legislators.
- Too much information was provided.
- Presentation was not well planned.
- The information was not reliable.

POLITICS TRUMPS MANAGEMENT

Not surprisingly, decisions to add or eliminate programs are more often spurred by political ideology than performance information and/or evidence of program success. In his November 2018 presentation at the annual Association for Public Policy Analysis and Management (APPAM) conference, Phil Joyce noted that of 170 reductions and eliminations in the Trump 2019 budget proposal, just forty-five "included citations from some source justifying the change.

"Under the most generous interpretation of 'evidence-based' roughly three-fourths of these reductions did not include such justifications," he wrote.[7]

Likewise, when Republican president George W. Bush tried to integrate the information in his management agenda and his Program Assessment Rating Tool (PART) into the executive budget, the Democratic Congress was not responsive.

Box 7.1 | Rx for Pitfalls

Following is a checklist of recommendations to optimize the use of performance management initiatives.

- It is important to acknowledge that performance management systems are an integral part of government—like budgeting or procurement—and not just an adjunct effort.

- Performance management initiatives are more likely to be sustainable if they are not overly identified with an outgoing political administration. It is better for them to be identified as a tool of the city than as "the former mayor's thing," says What Works Cities' Zach Markovits.

- The Urban Institute and others strongly recommend that narrative explanations are presented side-by-side with performance measurement information or other data. This provides the opportunity to put the numbers into context and to make sure that readers understand any exogenous factors that influence results. If numbers used in performance measurement systems are thrown wildly off by a forest fire, flood, or hurricane, for example, it is important to communicate that.[a]

© iStock/Getty Images Plus/seb_ra

- Communication of performance measurement information to legislators should be kept short and to the point to increase the likelihood that it is read. Knowledge of committee schedules and study assignments are extremely helpful in determining when information may be most useful and when it will overload legislators or their staff.

- Sharing experiences with individuals in other cities, counties, and states who are involved in performance management

(Continued)

Box 7.1 | *Continued*

efforts provides an ongoing support system and way to share ideas and experiences. We saw the benefit of what Maia Jachimowicz at Results for America calls the "fellowship model" when we attended Managing for Results conferences in Austin in the 1990s.

The ability to gather together with other people who are working in neighboring or even faraway governments and dealing with the same issues and frustrations has enormous payoffs. Many of the participants involved in What Works Cities or Results for America fellowship programs cite the benefits that they've received from their connection with other participants. The personal connections that grow out of participation in a network are also a fundamental part of the success of Washington State's Government Performance Coalition, which brings together twelve hundred local performance practitioners across the state.

• Building an organized information infrastructure can help both central offices and agencies know the work that has been completed in the past that may be relevant to current efforts. Central data inventories help managers know what information from other agencies would be useful to them. Centralized easy to access websites that provide retrievable copies of government reports and evaluations make sure that past work is not lost.

• Caution should be exercised when utilizing incentives as an inducement to meet performance targets. Too often, incentives, whether in contracts, pay-for-performance plans, or linked to increased funding, lead to gameplaying with performance results.

• The beginning of a new program or policy initiative is the best time to consider the data that will be needed to analyze and evaluate how well it is doing and what changes may be needed to make it work better.

• Building up workforce data skills is a pressing need that can be accelerated through both internal and external resources, with train-the-trainer and mentor relationships helping to spread the knowledge. Coaching is also needed to keep building skills among workers without technical training. Networks help to encourage participants to see performance management as a living, breathing process that they can support through their participation in training forums, strategic

conversations, and design workshops and that will break down silos, erase feelings of loneliness and fear of change, and bring joy to the performance management effort.[b]
- Performance management benefits from a dash of realism in what can be accomplished with the resources available. This means avoiding overexpectations and overselling of the initiative and not underprojecting staff and resource needs.
- The importance of building relationships between government and academia, with an emphasis on better communication on both sides, is already in the air. One example: a half-day forum that was focused on bringing policymakers and academics together in 2017, sponsored by APPAM and the Sanford School of Public Policy at Duke University. Some of the key messages included: (1) the need for safe spaces to have discussions without the threat of publicity, (2) a more systematic way for practitioners to know what research universities are currently engaged in, and (3) the importance of considering research needs at an early stage of a project rather than down the road.[c]

[a]E. Blaine Liner, Harry P. Hatry, Elisa Vinson, Ryan Allen, Pat Dusenbury, Scott Bryant, Ron Snell, "Making Results-Based Government Work," Urban Institute, April 1, 2001, www.urban.org/research/publication/making-results-based-government-work.
[b]Larisa Benson and Chelsea Lei, "Why We Need Joy in Government," MRSC blog, September 7, 2018, http://mrsc.org/Home/Stay-Informed/MRSC-Insight/September-2018/Why-we-need-joy-in-government.aspx.
[c]Barrett and Greene, Inc., "How to Get Universities and Governments to Work Together," March 21, 2017, https://www.greenebarrett.com/post/how-to-get-universities-and-governments-to-work-together.

8
Buy-In

■ ■ ■

THEORETICALLY, IMPROVING PERFORMANCE should be entirely satisfying. What could be a more fulfilling job than one that helps make the world—especially the world in immediate geographic proximity—a better place? But developing new management systems is almost always underresourced, frustrating, and time-consuming for busy government departments. As a result, the activities that feed the performance management effort, often imposed upon departments by central offices, can be resented by the people who are gathering, analyzing, and disseminating the data. Unless busy employees see the value of performance management to their own work, they may not appreciate that the extra effort required is anything more than a waste of time.

There are multiple consequences to a lack of buy-in. Data errors multiply when employees don't see the value of accurately recording or inputting their work. Program implementation of evidence-based policies may suffer from a lack of fidelity to the original model or a lack of attention as to how the model fits with local needs. Low engagement levels lead to higher turnover and lackadaisical employee performance.

Performance management is far more successful when there is buy-in up and down the ranks from lower-level employees who are gathering the data to those who are laboring at higher levels of the agencies.

RESISTERS

In the words of a Maryland policy analyst, "Bringing about any kind of change in state government is always a very difficult task. People get used to doing things in the same way and don't like to do things differently."

Longtime public sector workers often believe they can wait out new management initiatives because they will eventually go away like snow on the ground in spring thaw. Marv Weidner, whose Colorado-based consulting company, Managing Results, has worked with dozens of governments on performance management and cultural change initiatives, put it this way when he was still director of policy and strategic planning in Iowa: "People have been through a lot of management fads and they need to be convinced that this isn't one of them."

Sherry Schoonover, deputy IT director in Topeka, Kansas, is one of the key players in that city's performance effort. She noted that the tracking of performance measures by departments has been sporadic and that the defining of goals, which was left to the departments, has sometimes been difficult for them. She outlined some of the reasons for resistance to a variety of performance management efforts.

As she told us, "You have to make sure that the divisions and departments own this information; that they don't just report it for reporting sake. They really must understand why they are doing this. Does it make sense? It's not (just) about numbers."

One of the major reasons that public sector employees complain about performance management initiatives is the drain on their hours. The grumbling heard by the Topeka performance team was, "We already have enough to do. Why in the heck are you coming up with this?"

There can also be an unmistakable chilling effect. Efforts to make services more efficient can be interpreted as ways to save and cut staff. "Many individuals who work in a government are frightened when it comes to technology," says Schoonover. "It scares them. 'You're going to come in and automate what I'm doing, take it from eight hours to two hours, and my job will be eliminated.'"

The fear factor also showed up in a 2017 study about quality improvement offices in government agencies, prepared by CPS HR Consulting and the American Society for Quality's government division.

Larisa Benson has become a strong believer in putting less emphasis on managerial accountability and more on collaborative problem-solving. She now hosts a consortium of local performance managers in Washington State and was director of government management and performance under Gov. Christine Gregoire. "As soon as the brain goes offline because you're scared, your creative energy is gone," she says.

The study of Lean Process Improvement and Continuous Quality Improvement in government found that 20 percent of state agencies had a formal Lean quality improvement program in place. But it noted that the life span of quality initiatives tended to be relatively short, lasting around three to five years. Sustainability was hampered by a lack of "structured support" from political leadership and from agency leaders.[1]

A small survey that was part of the study found a high level of successful efforts—about 75 percent of improvement opportunities had solid records of implementation. But it also found that a lack of staff resources and staff fear were barriers. About 27 percent of respondents voiced a concern over possible loss of jobs from quality improvement activities.

Among the study's conclusions:

A number of significant barriers to the success of Lean Process Improvement teams exist and limit both the development and adoption of improvement opportunities. Most significantly, employees of units considering Lean Process Improvement are sensitive to the fact that their efforts could reduce the numbers of positions required or result in budget reductions in their agency, and specifically in the office in which they work. Those who manage these agencies must ensure that those who create process improvement opportunities know they will not lose their own job as a direct result or the root causes of inefficiency will never be revealed.[2]

ACCOUNTABILITY VERSUS PERFORMANCE IMPROVEMENT

Steve Kelman is Weatherhead Professor of Public Management at Harvard University's John F. Kennedy School of Government. When he teaches performance measurement, he distinguishes between the two very different interpretations that government officials apply to that subject.

"When I teach performance measurement at the Kennedy School, early on I discuss two different words that might come to a government official's mind when they hear the phrase 'performance measurement.' One is 'accountability,' the other is 'performance improvement,'" he wrote in a blog post in October 2018.[3]

Managers' reactions to these very different concepts are somewhat predictable. If the emphasis is on accountability, "their reaction is likely to be negative," wrote Kelman. That's because the notion of accountability carries with it a "gotcha" ethos; succeed or face negative feedback from supervisors or even impediments to career progress.

"On the other hand," Kelman argues, "if the emphasis on accountability is supplanted by aiming toward performance improvement, managers are likely to embrace the effort. So, in arguing for an association of performance measurement with performance improvement, I am fighting to give people a positive association with the concept, not a negative one."

In his work in Missouri in the mid- to late 1990s and his subsequent intensive work with human services agencies, Ken Miller has seen the negative impacts of an overemphasis on accountability. When individuals are held responsible for the outcomes of their work in a field in which multiple external factors influence outcomes, he sees data becoming vulnerable to manipulation. "If you are held accountable for what is out of your control, the recourse [may be] to game the system," he told us.

Despite his logic, performance measurement and evaluation are still assembled for accountability purposes, which can cause employees to run in the opposite direction. "There's no shortage of data that is collected because someone else wants to justify spending or spending reduction," he says. "It's not data that answers the questions that employees in an agency have. It's almost always data that someone else wants."

AGENCY OWNERSHIP

Rigorous performance management systems are most likely to succeed when the agencies involved, and the employees within those agencies, can see a direct connection between the systems that are being put in place and the success of their own work.

Making this connection for agency employees and for those who work in Colorado's sixty-four counties was one of the fundamental principles that contributed to the success of the Department of Human Services C-Stat system during Governor John Hickenlooper's administration, between 2012 and early January 2019.

C-Stat asked a great deal of the workforce. Director Reggie Bicha and performance chief Melissa Wavelet had five meetings a month, one for each of the five programmatic offices within the Department of Human Services, to go over C-Stat data. A report written in early 2019 by Wavelet for the IBM Center for the Business of Government explained how everyone was expected "to clear calendars to prepare for and attend the C-Stat meeting." It was not in addition to the "real work" but represented "the real work," she wrote.[4]

C-Stat also required time-consuming and work-intensive attention to performance measurement, data analysis, and evaluation for the state's sixty-four counties. Fully engaging the counties required that they perceived the new central office demands as making their own work more successful, not just as an exercise in compliance. "They became consumers of their own performance data," according to the report.

One of the outgrowths of C-Stat was a county Performance & Partnerships Exchange, a "peer-to-peer learning method for counties focused on improving performance on county-administered programs as measured by C-Stat." The exchange provided a way for counties to share successful practices with each other, learning how to improve their own work by benchmarking on each other. (See Q&A with Melissa Wavelet on page 92.)

STAT EVOLUTION

Although the C-Stat program in Colorado has been very successful and appears to be continuing in the new administration of Governor Jared Polis, it required very committed top leadership to drive change. One of the hallmarks of its success was a commitment not to waste anyone's time or to use Stat meetings as a weapon with which to bully employees.

Other governments have found their original Stat approach to be too time-consuming and difficult to sustain, given the many demands on leadership and public sector worker time. Agencies rebel when the accountability element is overemphasized, and managers are caught unaware by surprise questions about data anomalies or missed targets. "The major criticism of the Stat meeting is it is a gotcha conversation," says Zach Markovits, director of city progress at What Works Cities.

© iStock/Getty Images Plus/Tero Vesalainen

In countless recent interviews, we heard similar stories from city and county managers who are changing their approach from Stat-style top-down data meetings to a gentler, more collaborative, format.

A bit of background: Following the introduction of CompStat in the New York City Police Department in the mid-1990s and the subsequent development of CityStat and StateStat in Baltimore and Maryland, Stat programs blossomed around the United States.

In nearly thirty years of observing government performance management efforts, we have rarely witnessed so many adherents grab onto an idea with such unbridled enthusiasm.

It is not surprising that CompStat was quick to gain national and worldwide attention as its tactical and strategic approach to crime-fighting had an immediate impact on New York City's crime statistics. Launched in 1994 by NYC police commissioner William Bratton and his deputy Jack Maple, whose brainchild it was, CompStat's much-replicated approach used frequent intense department meetings to analyze crime data, compare precincts, and drive down spikes in crime through targeted enforcement activities (see photo 8.2). One of the hallmarks of CompStat was its focus on the individual responsibility assigned to operational unit commanders, precinct chiefs, and other police department officials for bringing crime rates down. Bratton's photo appeared on the cover of *Time* magazine in 1996 for his work (although rumor had it that Mayor Rudolph Giuliani resented the national attention that his employee garnered).

While other societal and demographic factors were also involved in the city's changing crime picture, the post-CompStat decline in crime in the late 1990s was hard to ignore. In 1993, there were 1,946 murders in the city. That dropped to 673 in 2000. The number of car thefts declined from 111,611 in the year before CompStat started to 35,422 in 2000.[5]

The CompStat approach, which is still used in New York City and in many other police departments, continues to have multiple advocates, but it has also generated negative publicity for creating an accountability pressure cooker.

We saw the negative aspects of the CompStat approach ourselves from a slightly unusual angle. When she was about ten our daughter played on a travel soccer team in Manhattan with a coach who was a full-time narcotics detective in the New York City Police Department.

Up until that point, we had heard only glowing reports of CompStat. how his colleagues in the New York City police department were so unnerved by the aggressive nature of the CompStat

CompStat in Action: New York City Police Continue to Analyze and
Use Crime Data.
New York City Police Department

meetings that some of them would be physically ill before they made
presentations. This coach was a detective in the narcotics division,
and it appeared that meeting with his superiors in a regime of fear
gave him a bigger case of the jitters than confronting a heroin pusher
in a dark alley did.

A COLLABORATIVE APPROACH

Maia Jachimowicz, vice president for evidence-based policy implementation at Results for America, has a core philosophy that it is a
mistake to be a slave to any set of specific performance management
processes or models. Still, she has observed a clear shift in how cities
are approaching the use of performance data.

"One model is we're in the same team and we'll solve this
together," she said. "The other model is I'm holding you accountable
for this whether or not you have the resources, ability, or time to
create change. Over time, many more jurisdictions are pulling away
to a more collaborative model."

Tulsa, Oklahoma, provides a good example of ways in which the Stat model is changing focus on challenges that can be solved in partnership and not by "putting people on the spot."

James Wagner was chief of performance strategy and innovation in Tulsa until February 2019, when he was named the city's new finance director.

Back in 2016, when he was asked by Tulsa mayor G. T. Bynum to be part of a team that put together an office of performance and innovation, he veered away from an accountability-oriented approach. Instead, he said, the new TulStat project became "more of a partnership about how we can use data and develop theories and track progress over time. We've seen ourselves as partners with the departments in implementing the work."

This was a seemingly positive advance, but even then, departments were not won over immediately.

One of the problems for the new TulStat approach was that it tried to do too much, too soon, having frequent meetings with multiple departments and covering way too much data. Even with a "partnership" approach, meetings gritty with numbers (many numbers) sometimes devolved into a "Gee, that's interesting" kind of conversation. A regurgitation of numbers meeting after meeting, without a real focus on how to get where you want to be, did not win the hearts of departmental partners, he says.

Sensing departmental resistance to the time spent in meetings (and preparing for meetings), the performance team shifted its approach.

There was one modest change: The new approach included a short survey at the end of each TulStat meeting to ask participants whether the purpose of the meeting was defined, whether action steps were clear at the meeting's close, and whether the meeting was a good use of the department's time. At each meeting the results of the survey from the last one that involved the same topic are shared. "We always show the data from the previous meeting so we're transparent," Wagner says. The performance team also has made it clear to the rest of government that they are flexible and open to changing how they do things.

Another shift in the Tulsa approach was to focus on a small group of problems with meetings held around problem topics rather than around a more expansive view of department measures.

One of the first problems tackled was police recruiting. Wagner: "For us, it has been a shift from focusing on the data to focusing on the problem. In police recruiting it was one thing: We wanted to get thirty candidates in every single class.

"The data became a flashlight to understand the problem. The focus of the meetings isn't data, data, data. It is solving a problem."

To improve the recruiting process, the performance team worked with the department to map out the steps that were followed in producing new police officers. Although the police department had been missing its police recruiting targets, the fact that the targets were missed was never the focus of the meetings.

Instead, the performance team worked with police to use data to figure out where the bottlenecks were in the recruiting process. Data analysis showed that the department was generating plenty of interest, but that applicants weren't completing applications. They were falling off at the point that they had to fill out a massive paper form that required them to produce an enormous list of people they knew and where they had lived. When the project was started, Tulsa had money for a class of thirty new cadets. But it only was able to fill the class with seventeen individuals. "We had plenty of applicants, but they didn't fill out this form," says Wagner.

As a solution, the performance team and the police department settled on the idea of having a major in the police department leadership call applicants directly and encourage them to complete all the steps in the application. This personal touch replaced an auto-generated email and it worked, bringing the cadet class to a nearly full twenty-eight-person enrollment. With staff shortages a major problem for Tulsa's police, the collaborative effort changed the way the police department reacted to the performance and innovation team.

The shift in the performance team approach from focusing TulStat meetings on a broad look at departmental performance measures and underlying data to focusing on specific department problems won over the police department, which is now recommending the performance team's involvement to other departments. "We've gone from reluctance to them recommending doing this to move the needle on a problem," says Wagner. "I didn't think I'd ever hear that."

CASE STUDY

Colorado Q&A on Achieving Buy-In

For five years, Melissa Wavelet headed the Office of Performance and Strategic Outcomes at the Colorado Department of Human Services (CDHS), where a Performance Stat approach was adopted in 2012 to improve outcomes across the large state agency. The approach, known as C-Stat, created an ongoing data-driven dialogue to improve services delivered by more than five thousand state employees, hundreds of contractors, and sixty-four counties that administer human services in Colorado. Although some state and local

Melissa Wavelet
Courtesy Melissa Wavelet

Stat programs have lost steam in the last few years (see page 87), C-Stat was able to work through many of the challenges and remains a center-piece of the department's approach to managing performance in 2019.

Wavelet left Colorado government early in 2019 when Gov. John Hickenlooper's term ended. Following are her observations of how the central executive office was able to get buy-in from internal state employees, contractors, and county partners.

Q. **What are the most important ingredients to get staff buy-in to a time-consuming and intense performance management/measurement program?**

A. You have to want to learn and sometimes that's scary, especially in human services where you find abuse and neglect, underperformance, noncompliance, and all sorts of ugliness that you'd rather not discover. You have to have the willingness to find ugliness and recognize that it is not a reflection on you as a leader but a reflection of the challenges inherent to human services.

That's a leadership thing. The leader sets the tone of what matters. Governor Hickenlooper set a tone that valued measurement. CDHS director Reggie Bicha excelled in that environment and relied on C-Stat to develop, manage, and improve key measures of success, which typically coincided with what matters most to our customers.

Q. Did the legislature pay attention to C-Stat?

A. If you wanted to get legislative laws or statutes changed or get additional funding, you'd have to make a solid argument. C-Stat facilitated the diagnosis of performance problems, the analysis to identify potential solutions, and a venue to discuss whether the identified strategies were working or not and why. Since C-Stat was part of regular CDHS operations, legislators were aware of it and would routinely ask how it had played a role in our thinking behind proposed legislative or budget items.

Q. We've seen in many states and cities that elected officials are suspicious of performance measures—they don't really trust the data from the executive branch. Was that a problem?

A. Just as the legislature was aware of C-Stat, the legislative auditor would request C-Stat data and definitions when auditing our programs. At times, the department's approach to defining the numerator or denominator or setting the goal was scrutinized. This led to rich discussions of how the measure and goals reflected priorities and preferences of the executive branch that might not align with others' priorities or preferences.

But broadly the information was trusted. We published the C-Stat data every quarter in a public report, which is available to the media, the legislature, the state auditor—anyone interested in learning more about the system's performance on key indicators of success in Colorado's state human services system.

We were also up-front about data weaknesses and changes. Sometimes it's just incomplete or requires correcting retroactively as you get smarter about the data. Sometimes you just have to start with the data you have (warts and all) and be transparent. You have to point out where the data is lacking so it doesn't get misinterpreted.

Q. What kind of personality characteristics contribute to success in a system like the one that was created in Colorado?

A. Curiosity is the most important characteristic—being curious and open-minded, eager to learn, and interested in improvement. Managers who work well in this environment serve as great role models for their teams. The teams have the analytic capacity to identify performance deficits and then figure out which strategies are most likely to address them. They don't see themselves as passive victims of this approach or of the sometimes-challenging dialogue in monthly C-Stat meetings.

That means they're not afraid that there are things that aren't working. They're less afraid of failure or mistakes. They know that everyone in the C-Stat meeting is committed to tackling the problems together.

Q. We know the frequency of the meetings for C-Stat caused some griping. Can you comment?

A. The performance unit and the executive leadership held ninety-minute meetings every Wednesday. And once a month, we'd hold back-to-back ninety-minute meetings since we had five programmatic offices. This monthly schedule translated into very short time frames for the production of the slide deck, action items, and materials. This tempo created a sense of urgency and was a source of stress. To be effective, program leadership had to make C-Stat part of their routine operations and couldn't ignore it in between monthly meetings.

Not only is the pace of business quite fast in a large human services agency, there are frequent interruptions, crises, and distractions. Colorado's annual budget development process, combined with the five-month legislative session, requires attention that can detract from any performance management approach. The monthly meeting cadence kept focus on what matters most for our customers, our stakeholders, and our funders. Although less frequent meetings can still serve a good purpose, the risk is they become perfunctory and less action-oriented.

Q. **Was there any disagreement about what data should be collected or what the central office wanted to measure?**

A. Of course. Which data, measured in which way, and, probably most importantly, which goal could be controversial. And, it wasn't uncommon for a goal to get more ambitious over time. We would achieve the 85 percent target for six consecutive months and rather than retire the measure to the dashboard where it received less examination, leadership would propose raising the goal to 90 percent or 95 percent. We were often ratcheting up the goals. That expectation was sometimes tiring to people. There's a fatigue around always striving for more, and after several years of examining the same measure, the performance management unit begin studying the notion of "performance fatigue" and how to combat it. We would debate when is performance "good enough," and the needs of the child, troubled youth, intellectually disabled adult, elderly veteran, and others we serve were always considered in that debate.

Q. **You developed ways to recognize the staff across the department and in the counties. How important was that?**

A. I think recognition is very important for any performance management effort. Leadership granted the first C-Stat award in March 2013 with cupcakes, certificates, and a modest, one-time financial payment to staff who were behind the improvements. By 2019, there were twenty-two C-Stat awards granted to state employees and contractor staff, making them somewhat exclusive and a good motivator. Counties also receive annual awards for sustained achievement of goals for the services that they are responsible for delivering (approximately twenty measures). CDHS director Bicha reflected that "the County C-Stat awards were a game changer. ... Recognizing them got their attention."[6] They created good will with staff and counties, and it shows that hard work matters and small wins matter. That was how I got to see a lot of the state. Leadership would travel to the county; sometimes it took eight hours to get to the corners of the state from Denver to spend a few hours in the county offices giving out certificates to the staff who were identified as responsible for making the program improvement. The event would sometimes get positive local press and praise from local elected officials. The time and attention invested in these trips reinforced the department's commitment to performance improvement and C-Stat as a strategy.

9

Validation

■ ■ ■

"DATA QUALITY NECESSARY to support detailed analyses is usually uneven at best," reported the Pew Charitable Trusts in February 2018.[1]

Few twelve-word sentences could, at heart, be more chilling for the men and women who are engaged in advancing performance management work. While the use of data in government is expanding dramatically each day, much of it is inaccurate, untimely, unfocused, siloed, and hard to use.

If you consider a useful performance measurement system as a huge structure made of bricks, the data is the mortar. If the mortar is flawed, the building can become dangerous to all occupants.

Performance auditors at all levels of government uncover data problems on a regular basis. "We often find bad data. Agencies collect data for administrative purposes and trying to translate that to data that can be used to measure performance is not always easy," says Joel Alter, director of special reviews for the legislative auditor in Minnesota.

With the advantages of new technology, you might be led to believe that the quality of data would be improving steadily. But the technology that makes the accumulation of data far easier, leads the list in many entities as a problem in coming up with accurate, timely and useful information.

Moreover, undertrained workers, and inconsistent definitions for specific data points, contribute to a fog of numbers that make it difficult for astute public sector decision makers to rely on data for making decisions.

The problems of poor public sector data are becoming more urgent as data is increasingly used to solve city, county, and state problems and improve performance. "If you want to use data for designing interventions, evaluating impact, and sharing and developing new insights, the challenges of poor data quality become more pronounced," says Stephan Verhulst, cofounder and chief development officer of the Governance Laboratory at New York University.

CONSEQUENCES OF BAD DATA

One of the consequences of shaky data: distrust by decision makers.

It would be a foolish legislator who relied on uncertain information to make decisions. In years past, this has been the problem with making policy based on a particularly rich anecdote that isn't representative of the city, county, or state, like a heinous murder that leads to a change in sentencing policies. But misleading data, however persuasive gritty charts and tables may be, is an equally improper source for leaders.

The impact of misleading data on individuals who are served by government programs can be particularly devastating at the ground level.

In 2016, for example, a California audit criticized the state's departments of Social Services and Health Care Services because of the incomplete information on prescriptions for psychotropic medications. Neither department could identify from the data which foster children were prescribed which medications. Poor data quality contributed to what the auditor described as a failure of the state and its counties to adequately oversee medication prescriptions for the children under its care. That meant that many children in a foster care sample from Los Angeles, Madera, Riverside, and Sonoma were receiving psychotropic medicines "in quantities and dosages that exceed state guidelines."[2]

That same year, a Kansas audit critiqued state foster care data, saying that information about the number of available beds and licensed homes was spotty, with missing and outdated information. Numerous inaccuracies were found in the addresses of children in custody. Poor data meant that the Department for Children and Families did not have available information to match children with the most suitable home, make placements tied to a child's needs, or keep children placed close to a child's original home.[3]

A 2018 Oregon performance audit on the same topic found that the state lacked "crucial data regarding how many foster placements are needed and the capacity of current foster homes, inhibiting the agency's ability to fully understand the scope of the problem." The audit cited "uncertain and untested data integrity and accuracy, incompleteness, data entry errors and poor-quality data conversion."[4]

Criminal justice programs are vulnerable to similar problems. In 2017, we interviewed Gipsy Escobar, director of research innovation for Measures for Justice, an organization that assesses and compares the performance of individual counties on criminal justice issues to advance understanding of local criminal justice in the United States. She told us that her organization constantly runs into data quality problems that stem from disparate county case management systems, inconsistent data entry, extremely weak reporting on racial disparity issues, inconsistent use of personal identifiers, and very poor quality information on pretrial detention.

BAD DATA AND DRUGS

According to a study by Christopher Ruhm in the August 2017 edition of the *American Journal of Preventive Medicine*, about 20 percent of death certificates in 2014 failed to identify the specific drugs involved in an overdose death.[5] Although death certificate data has been improving, there are still serious flaws.

"At the most obvious level, there's a question of targeting," Ruhm told us in spring 2018. Based on his work, opiate mortality rates drawn from death certificates substantially understated incidence in Pennsylvania, Indiana, New Jersey, and Arizona, while overstating it in Connecticut, Ohio, New Mexico, and South Carolina. Such errors can lead to misdirected funding. "We'd like to target resources to the places and to the groups that are having the worst experiences," he said.

Shortcomings in death certificate data were so extreme in some states that Ruhm's recalculations resulted in dramatic shifts in mortality rankings, moving the Commonwealth of Pennsylvania, for example, from the thirty-second-highest mortality rates in the country—a nice middle-of-the pack placement—to a far more alarming seventh place. Such basic errors can undermine any efforts at benchmarking the work in less successful venues on those that have made progress.

Ruhm stressed that a lack of drug specificity on death certificates, and other data quality problems, have helped to mask a resurgence of drug problems other than opiate abuse, which is getting a great deal of attention among policymakers. An increase in cocaine use and the potential impact of drug mixtures can easily be missed based only on information garnered from death certificates.

In April 2018, an article in the *American Journal of Public Health* written by a team at the Centers for Disease Control and Prevention (CDC) took a hard look at previous calculations of what the CDC had characterized as prescription overdose deaths. The article notes that illegally manufactured opiates were included in the earlier count and led to a substantial overstating of deaths attributed to opiates prescribed by physicians.[6]

Those calculations may have contributed to policy choices that overemphasized controls on physician prescriptions at a time when deaths from prescription drugs had already stabilized and illegally obtained drugs were continuing to increase.

INCONSISTENT COMPARISONS

How long does it take to respond to a call to the police or the fire department? How many minutes (or hours) do typical clients of Departments of Motor Vehicles spend in line? These kinds of measurements are often used by governments. But the differing details of how response time is measured can cause problems.

David Ammons, professor of public administration at the University of North Carolina at Chapel Hill, says citizens may assume that response time for a 911 emergency call is measured from the point that the call comes in.

In some places that's the case. But in others, response time is measured when the dispatcher connects with police, fire, or EMS, not when someone calls for help. First responders may prefer to use a measure based on the time of dispatch because they don't have control over the 911 call system. "But if they're doing that," Ammons says, "then there may be a problem with dispatch and the city council, and the citizenry are oblivious to that."[7]

The City of New Orleans is currently working on a problem caused by the fact that some of the local services are delivered by another government. For example, the 911 call center is run by the New Orleans Parish Communications District, which also holds the 911 data.[8]

This has led to a situation in which the Emergency Medical Services (EMS) department in New Orleans has not been able to access fire department data and the fire department has not been able to access EMS data. That's unfortunate because those departments often work together to save lives on the same emergency scenes.

"EMS will know when they got the call and when they sent it to fire, but they won't know when fire got on the scene. Fire will know when they got the call transferred but they won't know when the call originally came into 911," says Melissa Schigoda, director of the Office of Performance and Accountability in New Orleans since November 2017. The city is now working on getting all of this information into its central server, but until that happens the fragmented data inhibits analyzing response time performance.

At a March 10, 2018, American Society for Public Administration presidential panel on bad data, we told the story of how results can be skewed when data used to analyze government services are missing just one important element. In this case, the Portland ombudsman reexamined the data that had been used to assess the time it took to answer 911 calls. The time originally calculated by the Bureau of Technology Services had only included landline calls. When cell

Figure 9.1 Missing Information

Performance Measure	Bureau's Numbers (FY 2015–2016)	Corrected Numbers (Dec. 2016–Apr. 2017)*
90% of emergency 911 calls answered within 20 seconds	99.6%	67.8%
Average time to answer emergency 911 calls	1 second	23 seconds

Leaving out cell phone calls when calculating 911 call waiting paints an inaccurately positive picture of response. *The Bureau of Technology Services calculated five months with complete data at the Ombudsman's request.
Office of the Ombudsman, Portland City Auditor's Office

phone calls were included, the conclusions varied. The average time to answer a 911 call was recalculated from one second to twenty-three seconds (see figure 9.1). For a performance measure that called for 90 percent of emergency calls to be answered within twenty seconds, a 99.6 percent rate of success was corrected to 67.8 percent.[9]

DATA FUDGING AND OUTRIGHT CHEATING

The transfer of agency data to central information sources may cause agency managers to downplay less favorable data in their reports. This temptation may be amplified if performance measures and their underlying data are seen as a weapon that's being used to cut budgets.

Performance measures can be all too easily manipulated, with a wide variety of practices used to provide a more positive shading to less than pleasing results. Unfavorable data may be eliminated and programs may cherry-pick participants to accept only the clients whose needs are lesser than those of other potential clients—thus warranting higher success rates.

Graphic presentations of survey information can make positive change appear far greater than it really is, or downplay a negative outcome. Targets may be set irrationally low and measurement methods or data definitions may be altered.

From time to time, data fudging is just a cuddlier way to describe outright cheating, as when teachers and principals have been caught tampering with standardized test scores to make their schools look better. The most famous case occurred in Atlanta, with suspected problems surfacing in 2009 and culminating in a 2014–2015 trial in which eleven teachers were convicted by a jury of altering student scores.[10] In addition to the convictions, the scandal resulted in multiple resignations of teachers, principals, and administrators. According to media reports at the time, teachers and administrators were reacting to pressure to show good results or risk termination. There were also reports that successful outcomes resulted in pay bonuses that may have created incentives to change test scores.

Data falsification on standardized tests also have plagued schools in Baltimore, Cincinnati, Detroit, Houston, Las Vegas, Los Angeles, Newark, Philadelphia, and Washington, DC.[11]

Performance information is most often put in jeopardy when it is directly hooked to rewards and punishments for individuals who can manipulate the data in some way. For example, in 2014, a scandal erupted in the Veterans Administration (VA) based on the VA's efforts to reduce veteran medical appointment wait times by offering bonuses to administrators who kept waits limited to a fourteen-day period.

In 2014, multiple cases were uncovered in which administrators had gained those bonuses by altering the facts about actual wait times—in some cases by blatant falsification of records; in others by changing the way they measured wait time by hiding parts of the wait. There were different methods of altering the data. In one hospital, wait time was calculated based on the time between the first available appointment and the actual appointment. In that way, the period before the "first available appointment" was ignored.

There were other hospitals that kept two sets of records—one that showed the actual wait time for veterans and the other showing more favorable results that were shared with the VA.[12]

VERIFICATION

As the University of Maryland's Philip Joyce wrote in 2014, "If a performance culture is going to take hold in government, those of us who are advocating these reforms need to be realistic about the measures themselves and the incentives for people to misuse them."[13]

It might be sensible for cities, counties, and states to have a powerful oversight arm ensuring that the performance information that is being used is accurate and timely.

While some entities do, in fact, double-check the data used in performance management, there may be none that centrally undertake that task for all agencies. Topeka, Kansas, has at least fourteen hundred data sources and applications. Sherry Schoonover, the deputy IT director, is a core member of the performance team and puts an emphasis on data quality. She is responsible for validating data reliability, and that's a very good start. But still, she only has control of about 30 percent of the city's data. Departments develop data and data applications independently without necessarily telling the central office—"They don't want to ask for permission. They're afraid we may say no," says Schoonover.

For most state and local auditor offices, checking on data quality is a constant task as auditors, following professional standards, must assure themselves of the quality of data used to make audit judgments and to support analysis. When we interviewed auditors and evaluators in forty-six states in 2015 (see figure 9.2), we found that the most common challenges to accuracy are problems in data entry, a lack of documentation to support how data is collected or how different data fields are defined, data manipulation, untimely data, and insufficient protections of data, as well as incomplete and missing data.[14] (See box on page 106 for a look at the most common roots of inaccuracy.)

California's audit office has periodic data reliability reviews that look at the completeness and accuracy of the state's data. In its 2016 review, it found that of seventy-eight data reliability assessments, data were sufficiently reliable in thirteen, and not sufficiently reliable in twenty-two. For the remainder, the auditor's office could not determine reliability.[15] Longtime auditor Elaine Howle says a much better job needs to be done at documenting where data has come from and how it is collected.

Targeted evaluations or audits of the accuracy and reliability of performance measures are few and far between. Texas and Louisiana have

Figure 9.2 Auditors' Headaches: Disheartening Data Quality News

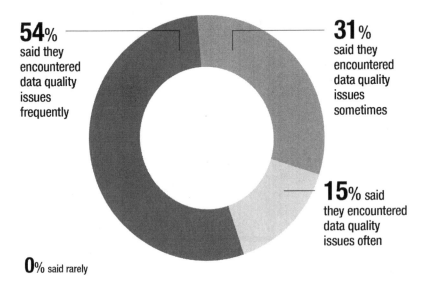

How Bad Is It? Over the past several months, *Governing* interviewed more than 75 public officials in 46 states who analyze data for a living. Each official was asked, "In your work, how often do you run into problems with data integrity, accuracy, availability or timeliness?" Fifteen percent of respondents said they were unable to generalize or couldn't answer the question. But of those who did, 69 percent said they "frequently" or "often" encounter data problems.

54% said they encountered data quality issues frequently

31% said they encountered data quality issues sometimes

15% said they encountered data quality issues often

0% said rarely

This graphic, from our 2015 *Governing* cover story about data quality, reveals the extent of auditor and other oversight officials' concerns with agency data.

done more than other states in looking at the legitimacy and accuracy of performance measures and the data that supports them. In a 2018 audit of performance measures at the Commission on Fire Protection, for example, the Texas State Auditor found it could not "certify" any of the six key performance measures used by the commission, concluding that it had weak information technology controls over its performance measurement data and "did not have sufficient controls over the calculation, collection, reporting, and review of data it entered into the Automated Budget and Evaluation System of Texas."[16]

Maryland's legislative audit office used to produce "managing for results" audits that labeled performance measures as "certified," "certified with qualifications," "inaccurate," or "unable to be certified." But when a new auditor came in about eight years ago, the performance measurement audits ceased. Now, the budget office takes on the task of keeping tabs on performance measurement validity.

Back in the 1990s, when Minnesota briefly had a requirement for agencies to produce annual performance reports, the legislative auditor's office routinely critiqued agency performance measures and the underlying data. When that law was repealed, data quality assessments became more sporadic. Says auditor Alter, "Now, when we do evaluation reports, we aren't looking at the full range (of data). We're looking at little pieces of it. Often as we do that work, we will comment on the measures that the agencies have and the adequacy of the data they collect."

A PATH FORWARD

Data becomes cleaner when departments recognize how useful it can be to them. Melissa Bridges, performance and innovation coordinator in Little Rock, describes the transformation undergone by agencies— like the city's Treasury Department—when they realize how useful cleaned-up data can be.

She remembers her early encounters with the city's Treasury Department. In a desire to be transparent, they had posted business license data on their website, but there was little standardization in the way they had collected the data. Names and addresses were sometimes keyed in half a dozen different ways, making it very difficult to identify businesses accurately.

The city's small performance unit showed the department how to clean up their information on business permits, utilizing other city data. One positive result for the department was that their business permit renewals ended up with far fewer returned envelopes for improper addresses. The cleaned-up Treasury data then became useful in other ways, as well—for example, matching it with other city data sets helped to identify business property owners who had outstanding code violations.

"They were sitting on a mound of dirty data, so we worked with them to clean it. They were so excited about it that they've gone through every other data set so that they can use it to make other improvements," says Bridges.

One of the big problems in validating data is that it is often difficult to determine from statute who has the final responsibility for that job.

Chief information officers generally oversee the technology systems but not the data that they produce. Technology managers often regard data quality issues as outside of their sphere of responsibility. "They don't think their role includes how consistent the data is," reported one program evaluator in a northeast state.[17]

A particularly promising advance has been the introduction of state government data officers who have responsibility not for the technology, but for the data that technology systems provide. Their roles vary, but generally include attention to data strategy, usefulness, collection, and reliability. Council of State Government research found these new positions in seven states in 2014. A report by the IBM Center for the Business of Government four years later reported the number had grown to eighteen. As of June 2019, there were twenty-three state chief data officers participating in the State Chief Data Officer Network, according to Tyler Kleykamp, the chief data officer in Connecticut.

The federal government's Data Act has also put in place new requirements that should eventually lead to major improvements in government information. Federal agencies are now required to put together data plans and attention to data quality is cascading down from the federal government to the states.

In addition, the GAO has the responsibility of reporting on the quality of information on USAspending.gov on a biannual basis. The first report, in November of 2017, found substantial quality issues.[18] The next GAO look at the quality, accuracy, and completeness of the quantities of federal data on that website was scheduled for November 2019.

In November 2017, the GAO gave leaders a lot to think about. The errors the GAO found—and there were many of them—show

how complex it is to make sure definitions used by scores of government agencies are consistent, that data reported about government awards matches agency records, and that the data behind $3.7 trillion in spending are recorded in a way that is complete. For example, in this first report following the Data Act, the GAO found that for the second quarter of fiscal 2017, data covering 160 financial assistance programs, representing an estimated $80.8 billion of annual spending, were missing.

Box 9.1 | The Roots of Inaccuracy

Over many years, interviews with state and local government officials have highlighted five of the most common causes of data inaccuracy.

Sloppy Data Input

Many individual state and local agencies lack strong controls to ensure the accuracy of data entry. Identifier numbers and dollar amounts are mistyped, for example. It is also reasonably common for "naming conventions" to be bollixed up. Sometimes a person's middle name will be used, sometimes a middle initial, sometimes an initial for first and second names, sometimes nicknames or names that are spelled in different ways.

Ineffective System Controls

Controls may be built into a technology system, but employees may find ways to subvert them. For example, a computer form might not allow a worker to move forward without a Social Security number, and rather than delay an application, the number input is 999-99-9999.

Inappropriate System Access

Many state and local audits cite the problem of unfettered access by too many employees to databases. For example, one New Jersey audit of the Department of Human Services found sixty-five separate individuals all characterized as "super-users" of the computer system. They had the ability to sign on to the computer, create electronic benefit accounts, issue benefit cards, and put money on those cards.[a] The fancy words for this issue pertain to "program integrity," but the ease with which data can be altered can be an open door to outright fraud.

Inconsistent Information and Missing Definitions

When state agencies depend on local governments, multiple school districts, or even regional offices, there is a danger of getting back inconsistent information unless a successful effort is made to ensure that data collectors are deriving the same information in the same way and using the same definitions. This is a particular problem when states rely on dozens of counties that are in turn relying on multiple nonprofits to deliver and code information.

Privatization / Contractor / Third-Party Issues

When government services are privatized, often the data available on performance is greatly diminished. This has been a problem with Medicaid managed care. A 2014 GAO report pointed out that neither the states nor the federal government had strong data on improper payments in managed care because just about all efforts to track improper payments were geared to fee-for-service systems. The report also noted that claims data in Medicaid-managed care were difficult to obtain and fell into a neglected middle ground on both federal and state levels.[b]

[a]New Jersey Office of the State Auditor, Office of Legislative Services, Department of Human Services, Division of Family Development, Administration and SNAP and TANF EBT Controls, December 4, 2014, 14, www.njleg.state.nj.us/legislativepub/Auditor/543213.pdf.
[b]US Government Accountability Office. Medicaid Program Integrity: Increased Oversight Needed to Ensure Integrity of Growing Managed Care Expenditures, May 2014, www.gao.gov/assets/670/663306.pdf.

CASE STUDY

New York: Changing the Definitions

In 2017, the New York City Department of Homeless Services experienced a sudden drop in "critical incidents," such as fights or weapons possession, in its Bedford-Atlantic Armory shelter. This housing facility is located in a part of Brooklyn that has recently been emerging from a highly undesirable neighborhood into one that increasingly attracts young college graduates in search of a livable neighborhood that still maintains remnants of affordability.

When the *New York Daily News* looked into the "surprising" results, it found the real reason for this allegedly good news. It turns out to be an easy matter to improve results by softening the definition of the things being measured.[19] If, for example, a city were to determine that it was going to give drivers a five-mile-an-hour leeway in making speeding arrests, overnight it could lay claim to making giant steps toward reducing speeding in its borders.

In New York, the definition of weapons possession had previously taken into account all manner of devices one resident could use to inflict harm on another. But the mayor's office changed the definition of a weapon, affecting the calculation of critical incidents. It still included firearms possession but not other weapons commonly found in shelters, such as knives, razors, and potentially lethal heavy objects nestled in socks to be used as an attack weapon.

Furthermore, even when a critical incident, under the new rules, was detected, the new guidelines left it a matter of judgment as to when it qualified as serious enough to be counted in the city's performance measures.

Officials of the Homeless Services Department believed that the numbers it was using before the definitional change exaggerated concerns about safety. But others saw the situation differently. "Though I can only state surely that the numbers are underreported," says Gregory Floyd, president of Teamsters Local 237, which represents employees in the department, "my speculation is that the city is underreporting numbers so it can show that the shelters are safer than they are."

The solution to this issue lies in greater transparency. Had the Department of Homeless Services provided a solid understanding of the data definition change to users of the measures, they would not have been misled, and could have used new measures appropriately, and not comparatively from year to year.

10

Data Progress

■ ■ ■

THE ADVANCES IN THE AVAILABILITY and potential utility of
government data over the last thirty years are undeniable, despite
shortcomings that stand in the way of progress.

Geographic information systems (GIS), for example, have long
helped cities deal with traffic and transportation issues and manage
infrastructure, but they are also increasingly used by cities, counties,
and states to analyze the equity of services and funding streams.

As noted in chapter 3, Indiana has been mapping the location
of drug overdoses with an eye toward matching problem areas with
better access to services. Similarly, Oakland County, Michigan, has
mapped data to see the location of opioid-related deaths and where
prescriptions are filled, charting the number of prescriptions written
per ten thousand residents in each part of the county. Through GIS,
it has also mapped locations where unused medication can be most
safely disposed. The creation of data maps provides easy access to
information for the wide variety of professionals who work to reduce
the county's substance abuse problems.[1]

For more than a decade, Global Positioning System (GPS) devices
have helped provide real-time data that can provide better sequencing
of traffic signals, redirect traffic flow, and save fuel costs.

Between 2008 and 2012, Delaware's analysis of GPS data enabled
it to save nearly a million dollars by reducing the miles driven and the

© iStock/Getty Images Plus/3DSculptor

fuel use of its fleet. The advances came from the data generated by installing GPS devices, which revealed both unauthorized vehicle use and excessive idle time.[2]

SERVICE DELIVERY

Data tools provide performance managers multiple ways to improve service delivery. Call center software, for example, enables managers to know the average wait time for a call to be answered and the percentage of individuals who hang up because they get tired of holding. This may not sound like an overwhelming issue, but consider the number of times you've heard people complain about waiting for long periods to get information from the state tax department. Armed with that information, managers can track back to the reasons for the delays and speed responses along. "There are things that are available today that weren't twenty years ago," says Joel Alter, director of special reviews for the Office of the Legislative Auditor in Minnesota.

Similarly, the ability to track the time spent by a health aide or visiting nurse in a home environment has provided new ways to monitor home health care. "Technology has transformed the industry. You can track how many minutes someone spends at each placement or each client down to the minute. It's revolutionized the way home care agencies track clients and report information," says Steven Rathgeb Smith, executive director of the American Political Science Association.

Among the most sophisticated users of data in the last several decades have been transportation departments. A growing number are using data to alter system design to prevent traffic accidents and communicate traffic danger spots to residents. For example, a number of cities around the country, in conjunction with the worldwide Vision Zero initiative, have used cameras and sensors to map out where even minor traffic problems occur in order to visualize traffic patterns and designs that will eliminate hazards.

In New York City, this information has led to new protected bike lanes and expanded medians.[3] In Tennessee, the highway patrol has combined data from past crashes with information on traffic citations, weather conditions, and other factors to determine the most dangerous areas at different times. This information is used to decide where officers should be stationed to control speeding or to locate checkpoints for sobriety or seatbelt use.[4]

At a more basic level, streamlined technology has helped performance teams to automatically access data from technology systems rather than forcing departments to hunt for data and manually pull out what they need when reporting on their performance information.

While many entities are still thwarted by outdated technology (see box 10.2), others see a dramatic change in the tools at their disposal. "With advancements in technology and data, we can move from aggregate measures that are not frequently updated to data that is granular, regularly updated, and useful for both operations and reporting," says Leah Tivoli, manager of innovation and performance for the budget office in Seattle.

In its two years of existence, the Tulsa, Oklahoma, performance and innovation team has advanced from using Excel spreadsheets and manual data to building "an entire business intelligence system to use data better," says Finance Director James Wagner. "We want to develop dashboards using computer systems to produce the data insights automatically (so) we don't have to spend hours putting together slide decks."

"There's been a data liberation over the last five or six years," says Beth Blauer, executive director of the Centers for Civic Impact at Johns Hopkins University.

OPEN DATA

One powerful resource to feed performance information to a variety of interested parties is open data. Over the last three years, Living Cities, in collaboration with *Governing* magazine, has invited cities to respond to a survey that assesses how they do in seven different "key outcomes of a well-performing" government.[5] One of those key outcomes looks at how data-driven each city is. In 2019, Grand Rapids, Michigan, came out on top, followed by San Diego.[6]

One contributing factor to this honor is that Grand Rapids has placed more than 80 percent of city data on its open data portal, with all city departments and agencies participating.

Its sophisticated data use helps Grand Rapids use mathematical modeling to measure how economic development has affected the displacement of people of color in gentrifying neighborhoods, with a data model showing how a neighborhood would look if proposed changes take place.

Grand Rapids' data on social determinants of health is used and available to determine policy related to lead abatement. Its open data portal helps the city work with external organizations that are developing apps. In civic hack nights, community members gather and experiment with a variety of tech solutions to solve city problems.

But there are also many cities in the Equipt to Innovate survey that are far away from making use of open data in sophisticated ways, with only 10 to 20 percent of city data in an open data format and no policies yet developed on how decisions on open data will be made.

"Open data is a sexy thing to do. But you can't do it unless you know your data inventory or what needs to be kept private or has sensitivity," says Zach Markovits, director of city progress at What Works Cities. "You can only really start having knowledgeable conversations if you know what data you have."

DATA SHARING

In some states, governors have aggressively promoted more common sharing of data among agencies. In Indiana in 2014, then governor Mike Pence created a central management and performance hub that provided a shared data environment, making it clear to agencies that the data generated through their programs was not theirs exclusively but was an asset that belonged to the state as a whole.

In 2018, Delaware governor John Carney signed an executive order that pushes agencies to contribute more data to the state's open data portal and encourages data sharing among agencies. That year, Oregon governor Kate Brown signed an executive order dealing with addiction treatment and ordering a wide variety of state agencies to share their data with the Alcohol and Drug Policy Commission.[7]

In the fiscal 2019 proposed governor's budget for Iowa, Governor Kim Reynolds pushed for increased agency data sharing in order to help government make more informed decisions. She also "expressed a desire to expand the use of data analytics through a new partnership with Iowa State University."[8]

The potential for achieving benefits from combined data sets is enormous.

If child welfare agencies have access to Medicaid data, for example, they can better identify higher-risk families and pinpoint the kind of help needed for targeted assistance. Job training programs benefit when they can access unemployment data, often a tricky proposition. As described in chapter 3, managers' ability to match family housing data with information on school achievement in Minnesota revealed the need to provide assistance to families of students who experienced homelessness.

Sadly, like so many of the provably worthwhile tools for performance managers, shared data is still more of an aspiration than a tool in many cities. The 2019 Equipt to Innovate survey showed that the path forward is not a steady or reliable one. The cities that respond to the survey may differ from year to year, but it is still disheartening that the 48 percent of cities that said they had interagency data sharing polices was lower in 2019 than either of the previous two years (see figure 10.1).[9]

In interviews conducted for the Pew Charitable Trusts' Data as a Strategic Asset (DASA) project, state officials discussed their concerns over ownership of data, problems with communication and coordination among agencies, technology hang-ups, a paucity of staff expertise, and a lack of resources to facilitate data sharing among agencies. Privacy concerns and fear of violating federal privacy laws were often mentioned as the reasons that agencies were reluctant to open up their information systems to other agencies or even to other departments within the same agency.

"Fear has been a barrier," says Jonathan Ladinsky, senior researcher for program improvement at Mathematica.

DATA GOVERNANCE

In the What Works Cities initiative, launched by Bloomberg Philanthropies, having solid data governance practices is one of the

Figure 10.1 Moving in the Wrong Direction: Grim News about Data Sharing

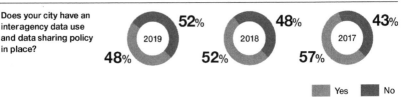

Does your city have an interagency data use and data sharing policy in place?

52% 2019 48%
48% 2018 52%
48% 2017 43%
57%

Yes   No

Governing, Equipt to Innovate Report, 2019

criteria for earning well-respected certification denoting excellence in city government.

Historically, though, governments have not been stellar in their efforts to establish governance structures to organize, review, and understand their data systems. "People run before they think about walking," says Markovits, at What Works Cities. "They jump into a Stat program, but they don't have data governance."

Over the years, one of the biggest difficulties in managing data and using it wisely has been the absence of leaders who were specific-ally responsible for data. Chief information officers have not routinely regarded this as their role, although more intentional data leadership has emerged with the rapid expansion of the chief data officer (CDO) position (see page 105).

One important task that faces governments—whether or not they have data officers—is building data literacy in their staff (see figure 10.2).

The performance team in Little Rock, Arkansas, has started run-ning mini data academies. By training employees to analyze and use data, they concentrate on specific problems and are careful to relate them to the human beings who depend on city services. "It's great that you have a mountain full of data, but we focus on getting employees to think about the resident, the human beings involved, and what the

Figure 10.2 Government officials' challenges in using admistrative data to improve programs and policies

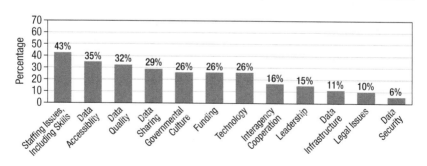

information means to them," says Melissa Bridges, performance and innovation coordinator there (see case study, page 120).

Still, the mini academy approach can only involve a limited number of people. Bridges wishes she had more time to do more hands-on training for frontline employees. "That's my big pain point right now. How do I do this internally without asking for another body? How do I leverage city tools and provide more internal training to our employees?"

"We need to double down on the skills of the public sector workforce," says Beth Blauer. The organization has provided technical assistance, networking, and training for 140 midsize cities around the world to help them leverage data and improve outcomes. It has now expanded its data academy so that individuals in other governments can participate for a fee.

Blauer and others still mention the negative effect that the Great Recession had on training and a wide variety of less formal continuous learning opportunities. When cuts were made to beleaguered

Box 10.1 | The Path Forward

To achieve better and more widespread use of data and data-driven decision-making, performance managers strive to:

1. Create greater ability to share data while also establishing privacy and cybersecurity protections.

2. Focus on staff capacity and training so that individuals within government know how to use the data at their fingertips and so that individuals with analytic expertise and ability are attracted to government jobs.

3. Continually improve the technology available to easily and painlessly collect, access, and analyze data so that time can be most productively utilized in performance management and not in tedious technical remediation activities.

4. Develop data that will focus less on compliance or accountability, and instead will facilitate learning and help provide the necessary clues to solve the myriad puzzles involved with serving a diverse population and doing it effectively.

5. Accelerate efforts to promote data governance to oversee and review the gathering and utility of this information to promote better decision making.

government budgets, training, as well as budgets for travel, conferences, and other networking and learning opportunities, were wiped out and remain shortchanged in many places.

Marc Holzer, executive director of the National Center for Public Performance, also saw training vanish in the budget cutting of the Great Recession when government funding tensions resulted in an antipathy to conferences, especially those that required traveling across state lines because of the perceived expense. For multiple years following the recession, he saw "no funding to buy books or journals or to keep information flowing," resulting in what he calls "a real innovation information deficit."

THE PUSH FOR MORE HELPFUL DATA

The increasing capacity of states to gather and manipulate large quantities of data has unquestionably improved performance management. In fact, in recent years the very term "big data" seemed to represent a magic wand to solve problems.

In a short twenty-person phone survey we did a few years ago, we discovered that the definitions of "big data" varied widely from government official to government official. And whatever "big data," means precisely, governments are still at a transitional stage for fully making use of the data they already have for analyzing problems and potential solutions, monitoring progress, and making better decisions.

One major challenge is that data still takes too long to emerge and, by the time it surfaces in this fast-paced world, the story it tells is often more about history than about a current situation. Public data dashboards, meanwhile, can reveal top measures but when decision makers want to dig more deeply into the numbers behind the numbers, they are frequently unable to do so.

In short, people who work in government communicate two seemingly oppositional messages: (1) they are drowning in the quantity of data held by their organization and (2) they are having trouble finding the data that they need.

In the 2018 Living Cities/Governing Equipt to Innovate report, only 19 percent of cities strongly agreed that "city data is easy for employees to access, consume and use in administering programs and planning."[10]

This problem may be more common in states than in cities, where much of the data is produced to satisfy federal compliance or accountability requirements or those imposed by state legislatures. The demands for compliance and accountability data leave less time for governments to actively go after the information that will help provide insight and further learning about programs.

The key question of what data can serve any individual program needs to be asked up-front, but often is not. Basic recidivism information—how many inmates are released from prison return within three years—is collected by every corrections department in the country. But a wide variety of information that could potentially cut down on recidivism is not.

"I don't think there is a jurisdiction in the country of any size that has even a quarter of the recidivism data that they want and need," says Adam Gelb, president and CEO of the Council on Criminal Justice, a nonpartisan policy and research organization.[11]

Box 10.2 | Outdated Data

Progress with data use doesn't come easily, and problems with technology systems have bedeviled governments ever since the days of cards with punch holes. One big drawback of unwieldy old systems is that they are inaccessible to the staff that could tap information for analysis.

As San Jose's Sharon Erickson told us, "We're gleaning information from different computer systems, some of which were devised in the 1970s."

In 2015, a team of researchers, including those from the University of Washington, NORC, Chapin Hall at the University of Chicago, and Mathematica Policy Research, looked at the use of administrative data in human services, interviewing about one hundred human service staff, as well as others who worked with them on their data. One of the issues discussed related to the problem recruiting staff to work with legacy systems. As a 2017 article in *Public Administration Review* explained:

> When staff members trained on these systems retire, it can be difficult to find young professionals capable of working within these dated systems. In these instances, capacity gaps are a function of finding properly skilled professionals, not funds or interest on the part of the agency.[a]

Even as governments enter the third decade of the twenty-first century, there are many departments in which workers are still using their technology as a way of collecting the data that was originally developed on paper.

The alternative, of course, can be mobile devices that allow field workers to gather information and feed it remotely into a government's data warehouses. But mobile devices are an expense and even in technologically savvy cities like Austin, you can still see field workers with pens and clipboards taking notes that will later have to be input into a computer database—a process that creates backlogs and errors.

Then, too, there are multiple computer systems in many governments. These are often reminiscent of the biblical Tower of Babel in which many hard workers attempted to create an edifice that would reach into the heavens but were punished for their hubris with the creation of many languages, so the workers couldn't communicate with one another.

Back from the scripture to contemporary cities, counties, and states, a variety of factors spur agencies to develop multiple individual computer approaches that don't communicate well with each other. Sometimes these have been dictated by the federal government, but they also result from the departmental yearning to procure systems on their own.

Antique and inaccessible computers also breed so-called shadow systems, where workers endeavor to create their own means for managing data, work that is often lost to other program staff and is certainly inaccessible to other departments.

Even when technology is upgraded, the shift creates temporary difficulties. One enticing benefit to governments that came along with the Affordable Care Act was a 90-10 split with the federal government on implementing new Medicaid Information Management Systems. Many entities were also able to include other related eligibility technology, but the upgrade from very old legacy computers and programs to new ones also caused a slew of problems.

In Washington, DC, for example, the promised upgrade contributed to a major slowdown in the already slow recertification process used for food stamps. In 2017, problems with the new technology system contributed to an alarmingly low 59 percent rate of certifications for the Supplemental Nutrition Assistance Program being done on time.[b]

[a]Scott W. Allard et al., "State Agencies Use of Administrative Data for Improved Practice: Needs, Challenges and Opportunities, *Public Administration Review*, 2017, https://onlinelibrary.wiley.com/doi/abs/10.1111/puar.12883.
[b]Meredith Roaten, "Judge says D.C. Government Delays Are Causing Serious Harm to Food Insecure Residents," StreetSenseMedia, June 28, 2018, https://www.streetsensemedia.org/article/snap-supplemental-nutrition-assistance-program-department-of-human-services-dhs-shonice-g-garnett-may-2018/#.Xc50_VdKiUk.

CASE STUDY

Little Rock: Of Data and Human Beings

There are lots of complex problems in state and local government that can take years to fix.

By breaking them down into pieces, governments can begin to deal with small problems that help solve bigger ones.

When Little Rock, Arkansas, started its new performance effort in 2016, it focused its efforts at the department head level. Says Melissa Bridges, performance and innovation coordinator for the city, "We didn't go to the people who had their hands on the processes day in and day out and who have a vested interest in making their lives better. That was a mistake."

So, the performance unit changed course to focus on mid-level employees. A good plan, but those employees still needed training. "Over the course of last year, that's exactly what we did. We hosted three internal data academies. We weren't showing them how to do mean, medium, and mode. We worked with our technology vendor, Socrata, to shape these academies around issues we needed to look at."

One of the mini data academies focused on how data could help improve quality of life in the neighborhood where their meetings were held. The building, an old repurposed school, was located in a struggling neighborhood. "The building is in the heart of the city. It's a neighborhood that is a food desert and has a high rate of crime," says Bridges. "That was our first focus. There was a crime issue, a food issue, and an economic development issue."

Data explorations started with a full analysis of code enforcement, census and crime data, demographics, and business locations. The 12th Street corridor, as the broader area is called, had lots of liquor and tobacco stores, but a paucity of food outlets in its six or seven distinct neighborhoods. Data analysis helped point Bridges's students to a neighborhood that had a particularly high crime rate and an older population, with high needs and more limited mobility.

To make effective changes based on the new information, they needed to get guidance from residents as well. A meeting was set up with the neighbhood association to find out what residents considered their biggest problem. Going into that meeting, the expectation was that the discussion would focus on dilapidated and neglected rental properties, absentee landlords, and high crime. "We assumed wrongly," says Bridges. "Their number one complaint was that the streets were too dark. There were a lot of streetlights out, which didn't give residents a feeling of safety."

Next step: Bridges's students accessed the city's GIS system, which showed where the streetlights were, but it did not show where they had gone out. On one Friday evening, the members of the data academy, along with some residents, canvassed the neighborhood. Of the two hundred light poles, forty were blocked by vegetation or were completely out. They then used the city's 3-1-1 app to lodge complaints so that the local electric company could cut back on the vegetation and replace nonworking lights.

The students learned some simple lessons about the use of data, and the neighborhood association was thrilled. They got real results for a problem that had nettled them for years. Subsequently, the same approach was taken in two other neighborhoods.

Solving the problem meant creating new data. "This wasn't something that the city was talking about as a performance measure," recalls Bridges.

"One of my mantras that I continuously preach: It's great that you have a mountain full of data, but think about the resident, the human being at the other end of that and what does the information mean to them."

City of Little Rock

11
Evaluation

■ ■ ■

TRADITIONALLY, STRATEGIC PLANNING and performance measurement help to guide government leaders and managers in the direction they want to head and then help them know how they are doing in reaching those objectives. "Performance measurement tells you what, but not why," says John Kamensky, senior fellow at the IBM Center for the Business of Government. "Evaluation tells you the why."

Evaluation is a rigorously conducted professional field with a well-thought-out list of competencies as spelled out on the American Evaluation Association website.[1] Other people who describe themselves as evaluators have a somewhat more informal approach. "Evaluation exists on a spectrum," says Jonathan McCay, lead program analyst at Mathematica.

The power of evaluation is undeniable. A look at ways to reduce the risk of adverse outcomes in child welfare programs was undertaken, for example, by the Idaho legislature's Office of Performance Evaluations.[2] As a result of this effort, major changes took place to improve the oversight structure, says Rakesh Mohan, executive director of that office. "That's the role of evaluation. If we don't do it, who else will?"

In the past, "we tended to have this attitude that on the one hand there was performance measurement and on the other, there was evaluation," says Paul Decker, CEO and president of the social science research firm Mathematica. "I think more and more these two concepts have become intertwined. We're blending with each other and the idea of frenemies becomes passé."

"You need both," says Donald Moynihan, McCourt Chair at Georgetown's McCourt School of Public Policy. "You need measures for a variety of purposes, and you need evaluation to understand the causal mechanisms. If you are only using one, it's like a bird flying with one wing."

Like Decker, Moynihan sees a thawing in the relationship of the different disciplines and growing integration that is a boon to the performance management field. This blending of disciplines is a work in progress and as Decker says, it is in a "nascent phase." In fact, there are a number of government institutions, particularly in state legislatures, that function very much like evaluation offices, but don't even have that word in their name.

ENOUGH MONEY? ENOUGH ATTENTION?

Notwithstanding the value of evaluation, however it is conducted, a lack of attention and resources has been a challenge.

In general, evaluation offices within state executive branches are in short supply, according to the *2018 What Works State Standards of Excellence* report from Results for America.[3]

"Evaluation resources" was one of fifteen criteria the report identified as needed by states to "consistently and effectively use data and evidence in budget, policy, and management decisions to achieve better outcomes for their residents." While Results for America has found that at least some federal agencies devote 1 percent or more of funding for evaluation, it could not find any states or state agencies for which this was true.

Looking across the fifty states, the report found only four states that had leading and promising evaluation policies in multiple agencies. For evaluation leadership, it identified only two states— Colorado and California—with senior leadership positions that had authority staff and budget needed for evaluating the state's major programs in order to inform policy decisions.[4]

Yet another problem often cited by experts is the lack of visibility that evaluations have. When the Pew-MacArthur Results First team explored how evaluation made its way into budget discussions in 2017, it found that in their 2013–2017 budget cycles, only thirteen states had included findings from program evaluations.[5]

Evaluations, whether they are produced by agencies themselves or by external consultants, can be hard to find, even by researchers who want to delve into the topic covered. They can be buried in layers of Internet web pages, with users stymied by outdated URLs and dependent on the vagaries of a Google search. To make evaluations more accessible, Results First recommends that a central repository be developed so that they can be easily located.[6] "Doing good studies and not communicating them is a waste of time," says Gary VanLandingham, who led the Results First effort from 2011 to June 2016, and is now professor, MPA director, and Reuben O'D. Askew Senior Practitioner in Residence at Florida State University.

Evaluation on the Frontlines

One of the frustrations voiced by practitioners about traditional evaluations is that they take too long. Those that are focused on long-term societal change may take years to complete and those that are looking at the impact of a program or the reasons behind its success or failure may not emerge until the program is complete or has been functioning for years.

"This is the beef I have with evaluators who only evaluate programs after they're finished," says Beth Blauer, executive director of the Centers for Civic Impact at Johns Hopkins University. "We have to radically redefine what evaluation means in government."

Blauer would like to see far more ongoing research and evaluation incorporated from the moment a program is conceived so that it is integral to program operation. This is a big change from retrospective evaluations in which conclusions may come years down the road, potentially affecting future programs but not in time to benefit the program that was studied.

She says the shift from a retrospective approach to one that is immediate and ongoing parallels that which occurred in performance measurement in the two decades that followed the 1980s. In the 1990s, attention to performance measures was often focused on the annual budget or annual performance reports that looked back on whether targets were met in the previous year. When the Stat movement took off, the attention was more regular and consistent. That's true also as Stat programs have evolved to focus, in a more collaborative way, on solving problems or achieving specific priorities. (For more on the evolution of Stat programs, see chapter 8.)

The change envisioned by Blauer and others "creates and cultivates an environment where innovation can take place to improve a program and then generate evidence that is of interest to the field," says McCay.

He sees a bottom-up approach rather than a top-down approach as an important development in evaluation and research, as they are increasingly used to develop evidence-based practices.

This means empowering local agencies, which tend to be the breeding grounds for innovation, so that they can see themselves as builders of evidence not just seekers of what has worked elsewhere. "We need to cultivate this and scale this," he says.

The idea is to start using data and information more intentionally to answer questions, using the broad range of research methods—qualitative, quantitative, descriptive, and statistical—on the ground.

In 2018, this kind of approach played out successfully in the Adams County, Colorado, Temporary Assistance to Needy Families program. A problem experienced there, and around the country, was getting clients to show up to scheduled orientation sessions and appointments after they had been approved for cash assistance.

The problem for families that were often dealing with a host of distractions and difficulties in their own lives was that the approval for cash assistance could be revoked if they did not show up. The problem for staff was a frustrating increase in workload as they endeavored to reschedule meetings and try various methods to get people to where they were supposed to be at the right time.

After studying the issue and the behavioral, social, economic, and practical factors that commonly contribute to poor attendance, the county, working with Mathematica, decided to implement a short-term experiment to see if a phone call and email contact in the couple of days before an initial orientation session could spur better attendance. To make sure that no other factors affected the result, parents who had been approved for cash assistance were randomly divided into a control group, which received no phone call or email prior to the meeting, and a group that got both.

This kind of approach utilizes the same basic methods as Randomized Control Trials (RCTs), often dubbed the "gold standard" of experimental design. RCTs provide comparisons between treatment and control groups, which allow researchers to see the impact of a new approach while minimizing outside factors that could lead to false conclusions about whether the "treatment" is responsible for whatever change is desired.

The rapid version provides a way to do mini experiments that can improve the management of programs with answers coming within months, not years.

The Adams County experiment went on for five months between January 3 and May 18, 2018. The results showed that the parents who were contacted in the two days before the orientation session had a 64 percent attendance rate, compared to the 51 percent attendance rate of the control group—the level of attendance generally. An additional effect was better attendance as well at follow-up one-on-one meetings with caseworkers—67 percent for the "treatment" group compared with 58 percent for the control group.

This simple way to increase attendance worked and in June became the policy for everyone.[7]

Multiple governments are embarking on low-cost evaluations. For example, in 2015, New Mexico's Department of Workforce

Solutions began a project designed to reduce unemployment insurance overpayments before they occurred.

Data analytics helped to pinpoint the part of the application process that was most likely to result in overpayment errors caused by potentially incorrect information from applicants. Then, working with Deloitte Consulting LLP, the state designed a series of "behavioral nudges" that popped up on an applicant's computer screen during the application process. By using a continuous randomized control trial approach, the department was able to see that some messages were more successful than others. As noted in a Pew Charitable Trusts brief on this initiative, a message that notified applicants that nine out of ten people in their county report earnings accurately was much more successful than a pop-up message that focused on the law and penalties for breaking the law.[8]

In 2019, New Orleans was embarking on a similar small evaluation, starting to try various behavioral techniques for getting residents to pay their water bills and traffic tickets on time. The aim was to measure the effectiveness of inducing payment when wording or graphics on letters changed.

This required randomizing customers so that some could form a control group. Getting this kind of approach launched does not happen instantly. It requires new skills on the part of departments that must use data in a different way than they have in the past. The water bill effort has been slowed, for example, as managers figure out how to accurately randomize customers—a task complicated by the way customer databases have been organized in the past, as well as previous billing methods that divided customers into multiple different billing cycles each month.

New approaches require culture change and provide both new tools and new roles to performance managers, who have not traditionally seen research and evaluation as part of their own jobs. Mathematica's McCay sees the potential for internal ongoing research and evaluation as actively supporting decision-making.

Box 11.1 | The Evidence Movement

Although resources for evaluation have not appreciably increased, much more attention and enthusiasm is emerging as the federal government, states, and local governments have jumped into using evidence-based policies and programs. The evidence upon which they draw is largely based on evaluations done by government entities, universities, consultants, nonprofits, or independent researchers. At least thirty-three states and DC have formalized the use of evidence through legislation or executive action, according to the National Conference of State Legislatures.[a]

In early 2019, President Trump signed the Foundation for Evidence-Based Policymaking Act, which is aimed at incorporating data and evaluation into program and policy decisions. In addition to calling for chief data officers for each agency, it requires that every agency has an evaluation policy, an evaluation officer, and evidence-building plans. The act was spurred by the final report from the Commission on Evidence-Based Policymaking in 2017.[b]

But as in all areas of performance management, big ideas can be difficult to implement seamlessly and without enough resources behind them. Says Kathryn Newcomer, director of the Trachtenberg School of Public Policy and Public Administration at the George Washington University, "The law is fine. The intent is good, but the interpretation and implementation are what I worry about."

The White House 2020 budget did not include money to help agencies put the new Evidence-Based Policymaking Act requirements into effect. "To make meaningful progress, some agencies are going to need more money," according to Nick Hart, director of the Evidence-Based Policymaking Initiative at the Bipartisan Policy Center,[c] a Washington-based think tank that promotes a bipartisan approach to policymaking.

Multiple experts have expressed concerns about implementation. Critics worry that the recommendations of the Commission on Evidence-Based Policymaking were more focused on the production of data, underplayed the translation of big ideas into actual use, and did not focus enough on how new evidence-based approaches would interact with the 2010 Government Performance Results Modernization Act or multiple other government performance efforts.

There is also a shortage of attention to how the federal government's new efforts to focus on evidence will connect with improvements to state and local performance. "The blind spot to me in this strategy is that there's $700 billion of funding that gets delivered to state and local governments and $600 billion of that is tied to programs that touch people. The Feds can't succeed without state and local partners," says Kathryn Stack, now an advisor to many performance management and evidence-based initiatives in the federal government and states.[d]

The focus on evidence-based approaches has led to a proliferation of clearinghouses that provide information on programs that have gone through rigorous evaluations and are deemed worthy of replication. As with all tools available to performance managers, the devil is in the details. Some observers note that more attention should go to what doesn't work as well as what does and that a more sophisticated approach to evidence would recognize that approaches that are successful for some people do not work as well for others.

For example, in juvenile services, multisystemic family treatment and functional family therapy have resulted in Midwestern programs that show success when evaluated, "but we couldn't get it to work in Baltimore," says Beth Blauer, who started her career in government as a juvenile probation officer.

Shelley Metzenbaum, whose work in many aspects of performance measurement and management has spanned decades, was associate director of performance and personnel management at the Office of Management and Budget during the Obama administration. She is married to Harvard professor Steve Kelman, Weatherhead Professor of Management at Harvard University's Kennedy School of Government.

In an article they wrote together for *PA Times* in 2018 they identified themselves as strong believers in the idea that programs should be evidence-based, but said the approach was too often oversimplified and that far more work should go into how programs or policies affect different individuals, exploring why programs may be very effective for some people and not for others.[e] The future of evidence-based practice in government, says Metzenbaum, parallels the arrival of designer medicine in which patients are accepted as individuals who will respond differently to treatments.

"One of the challenges with evaluation is that the way people define what works is what works on average. If you only look at what works or doesn't work on average, you miss the subset of adults who will respond differently," says Metzenbaum. "There is an increasing appreciation that this is important."

[a]Allison Hill, "It's the Law: New Report Highlights States That Highlight Evidence-Based Programs," The NCSL Blog, National Conference of State Legislatures, May 22, 2018, www.ncsl.org/blog/2018/05/22/its-the-law-new-report-highlights-states-that-mandate-evidence-based-programs.aspx.
[b]Commission on Evidence-Based Policy Making, CEP Final Report: The Promise of Evidence-Based Policymaking, September 7, 2017, www.cep.gov/cep-final-report.html.
[c]Chase Gunter, "Can Agencies Implement Evidence-Based Policymaking without Money?" FCW: The Business of Federal Technology, March 15, 2019, https://fcw.com/articles/2019/03/15/evidence-based-policymaking-budget-gunter.aspx.
[d]Kathryn Stack retired from the federal government in 2015 after thirty-four years working on management initiatives, most of that time in the Office of Management and Budget. For several years, she served as vice president of evidence-based innovation at the Laura and John Arnold Foundation and is now a consultant and a frequent advisor to OMB.
[e]Shelley Metzenbaum and Steven Kelman, "Doing Evidence Right," PA Times, January 8, 2018, https://patimes.org/evidence/.

Box 11.2 | A Cost-Benefit Approach

Using evaluations, and various kinds of cost-benefit (or benefit-cost) analysis, to figure out whether investments in programs succeed is a not a new idea. The State of Washington was the state pioneer in this field, with the establishment in the 1980s of the Washington State Institute for Public Policy (WSIPP). Over many years, WSIPP has utilized benefit-cost analysis to look at the benefit-to-cost ratios for different programs in a wide variety of fields including, juvenile justice, adult criminal justice, child mental health, child welfare, and substance use disorders.

These explorations use literature reviews and meta-analysis to tap multiple program evaluations and research studies and apply the results to Washington programs or proposed programs. For example, when WSIPP did a literature review of vocational education in prison in 2016, it calculated a $11.95 return for every dollar spent, while an exploration of life-skills education in adult criminal justice that same year found costs outweighed benefits by $1.39.[a]

The Pew-MacArthur Results First initiative has adopted Washington's methods and provided technical assistance to twenty-seven states, first in the criminal justice area and more recently adding child welfare and behavioral health to facilitate similar analyses of programs so that those with more positive results can be replicated and expanded.

In 2014, the Results First initiative defined the five elements needed for evidence-based policymaking, program assessment, budget development, implementation oversight, outcome monitoring, and targeted evaluation.[b] There's a good deal of overlap between these categories, but they emphasize the important role that evaluation plays in the drive to base programs and policies on past evidence of success.[c]

---

[a]Washington State Institute for Public Policy. Benefit-Cost Results. www.wsipp.wa.gov/BenefitCost.
[b]Pew Charitable Trusts/MacArthur Foundation, *Evidence-Based Policymaking: A Guide for Effective Government*, www.pewtrusts.org/-/media/assets/2014/11/evidencebasedpolicymakingaguideforeffectivegovernment.pdf.
[c]We served as senior advisors to the Pew/MacArthur 2014 Evidence-Based Policymaking report.

CASE STUDY

Los Angeles: How to Recruit Police?

New teams run by chief performance officers and chief innovation officers are increasingly making informal on-the-spot evaluation a part of government management.

In Los Angeles, the innovation team was launched with a grant from Bloomberg Philanthropies and after three years was retained and funded through the city budget. Now, in its fourth year, it has a six-person staff with its office located near a four-person data team and a small performance management team. "We all work together, but our tasks are different," says Amanda Daflos, the city's chief innovation officer, who serves as senior director of the innovation and data group.

One of her roles is to solve puzzles, using both quantitative and qualitative ways to uncover how city efforts could be improved.

In early 2018, her team tackled the difficult issue of police recruiting, a problem that is coming up in multiple places around the United States. As in many local governments, Los Angeles leaders were deeply interested in increasing the number of applicants to the city's police department, and in encouraging a more diverse applicant pool.

This was not a new idea. It has been a city goal for years, with one hopeful means of outreach focused on connecting with young people.

To that end, Los Angeles had launched a robust set of after-school programs that were designed to engage teenagers from diverse backgrounds in learning about the police and getting a sense of what life on the police force could be like.

But here was the conundrum: "We had seven thousand young people in youth programs all related to policing. The idea was this was a great way to engage young people," says Daflos. "But we learned that only a handful go on to become police officers."

The initial foray into finding a solution came from talking with human resource officers and the police department and from carefully studying the data. But that was only the starting point. The innovation team in Los Angeles is guided by human-centered design principles. A fundamental aspect of its efforts to evaluate a problem focuses on the way the program in question affects the people it is designed to serve.

The next step after exploring the department perspective and thoroughly understanding the data, was to talk with the human beings at the center of the question.

Sometimes, an exploration like this comes up with answers that seem almost obvious in retrospect. Through interviews with young people, focus groups, and surveys, the innovation team learned that one of the big problems was that young people left the introductory programs at age eighteen but could not apply to be police until age twenty-one. In the meantime, they went in other directions—to further their education or to take other, often low-paying jobs, for example, in fast-food outlets. "They needed a salary and so they'd go to work for Burger King. That was one of the roots of the problem. They might want to become police officers, but they needed a salary to provide support for their families," says Daflos.

The result of the innovation team's research was to set up a program called Pledge to Patrol, which was open to high school graduates between the ages of eighteen and twenty-one. These police apprentices were hired by the department as associate community officers at a part-time salary that enabled them to continue their involvement with police and learn on the job.

The apprentices were sent to work for different precincts, which provided them with assignments, some more imaginatively than others. By keeping close touch on the program through surveys every six weeks, changes were adopted in real time as it was being developed. The innovation team found that one early problem with Pledge to Patrol was that captains were confused about what to do with the apprentices in their charge and often overassigned desk work, which was not how the program was supposed to function.

The innovation team's solution to that issue was to provide more input to police stations on creative ways that apprentices could be put to work, help the department, and continue to view law enforcement as a good career choice.

Of the apprentices in the Pledge to Patrol pilot program, about 85 percent went on to apply to become police and nearly all were accepted. A proposal to expand the program to more young people is being debated as part of the 2020 Los Angeles budget.

"If we're spending money on something, shouldn't we know how it's going?" asks Daflos. That ability to explore questions internally and make changes to department design on an ongoing basis is helped by teams like hers that don't have ongoing departmental responsibilities to keep the streets paved and the water running. "We can support departments in solving problems they don't have time to solve. That's really powerful," she says.

Resources

■ ■ ■

WE WANT TO SHARE SOURCES we find informative, useful, and
sometimes entertaining when we are gathering information about
performance management.

Here is a short selection:

- **The National Association of State Budget Officers** has an
  inventory of program data and evidence initiatives in the states
  that connect to budgeting. As of November 2018, the list had
  ninety-one separate initiatives, with eighteen falling into the
  category of performance-based budgeting. The other categories
  are: data analytics, evidence-based policymaking, performance
  management, and process improvement. NASBO intends to
  update the inventory on a regular basis. The inventory is available on the NASBO website, listed under Reports & Data, and
  labeled "Using Data and Evidence in the States."
- In 2017, ICMA launched **Open Access Benchmarking,**
  which collects data on a short list of eighty key performance
  indicators and fifty-four additional county measures. The
  jurisdictions participating in those efforts have helped select
  and refine the measures over the years, both eliminating measures deemed no longer relevant and emphasizing those seen
  as "core comparisons." ICMA also features a Performance
  Management page on its website.

- **Results for America** provides a wealth of information with multiple spots on its website geared to different aspects of performance management and different levels of government. Under the Tools and Resources tab, we would suggest heading to the "Standards of Excellence" web page, which has separate sections covering federal, state, and local government.

One of our favorite spots to look at on the Results for America website is under the "Our Work" tab and it leads to a host of information on "What Works Cities." Results for America is the lead partner among the five organizations that make up the "What Works Cities collaborative team. A hyperlink in the text under the What Works Cities head provides the forty-five criteria that Results for America uses to provide certification for entities excelling in "data driven, well-managed local government."

- The four other What Works Cities partners are worth website visits on their own. They are the **Behavioral Insights Team, The Harvard Kennedy School Government Performance Lab, The Center for Government Excellence (GovEx)** at Johns Hopkins University, and the **Sunlight Foundation.**

While we were writing this book, a new umbrella organization was launched at Johns Hopkins, which is headed by Beth Blauer, who was formerly in charge of GovEx. It is called the Centers for Civic Impact and will contain GovEx, the GovEx Academy, and the new Center for Applied Public Research, which will "bring people together who are tackling the same types of problems to learn from each other," says Blauer.

- For individuals interested in evidence-based programs, through clearinghouses, the **Pew Charitable Trusts-MacArthur Foundation Results First** project provides a clearinghouse database. The Results First Initiative has also published a series of reports on the multiple elements that are needed for an evidence-based outlook in government.

- Reports and blog items posted at the **IBM Center for the Business of Government** are frequently written by well-known authorities. Although the focus is far more focused on the federal government, it does also venture into state/local topics— for example, the excellent report published about Colorado's C-Stat in early 2019. The Weekly Roundup is a good way of keeping in touch with federal performance actions and ongoing news connecting technology and data advances in performance. The best way to access the roundup and the center's other blogs is from the word blog, which can be found on the banner at the top of the website's home page. (In fall 2019, we became visiting fellows at the IBM Center and now have our own blog on that website, covering state and local isues, including performance management.)

We have relied on IBM senior fellow John Kamensky for decades to help us keep in touch with performance management advances (and declines) in other countries. Some of his past blog posts have covered New Zealand's "Results Programme," reform initiatives in India, and a comparison of citizen feedback in the Chinese city of Hangzhou and New York City.

- The **World Bank Open Knowledge Repository** provides links to reports and books on international performance management initiatives. A search for "performance management" on the website of the Organization for Economic Co-operation and Development yields a wealth of interesting international results.
- A few other suggestions: The **Urban Institute**'s multidecade work on performance measurement and management (search for those terms); **Actionable Research for Social Policy at the University of Pennsylvania**, which has a focus on the "development and use of integrated data systems"; and the **U.S. Census Stats in Action** videos, which show how different entities have used American Community Survey data to improve services.

- Of course, we also recommend the *Governing* magazine archives, which contain multiple past columns and articles by ourselves and others about performance management. This is a topic also covered by Route Fifty, where we are now senior advisors and columnists.

Glossary

∎ ∎ ∎

accountability: The process through which individuals or departments are required to take responsibility for any failures they encounter when attempting to accomplish their goals. Up to a point, ensuring that individuals, teams, or departments take responsibility for the fruits of their labors can be a useful exercise. Increasingly, though, there has been growing concern that too much emphasis on accountability can transform performance management into a "gotcha" exercise, which can have a chilling effect on progress.

benchmarks: One of the most powerful means of measuring performance is by comparing the outcomes in one state to another state or in one city or county to another. Benchmarking has twin advantages. It gives users information about other cities that are particularly successful at a particular effort and allows them to learn from the comparison. Additionally, benchmarking can serve as a wake-up call to those entities that find themselves rated as lagging their peers.

big data: A repeatedly used phrase in recent years, the amorphous term "big data" has generated widespread hopes in government that vast realms of data can be tapped through sophisticated technology to answer a wide variety of knotty policy questions. The term has different meanings to different people.

buy-in: Even the best ideas in government have little chance of gaining traction without the support of a variety of involved parties, often including the citizenry, the executive branch, the legislative branch, various commissions, employees, and so on.

citizen surveys: There are a number of outcome measures for services that can only be derived by going directly to residents to see how they would evaluate quality. For example, while it may be an easy matter to keep track of the number of new lampposts built in city parks, only a citizen survey can provide insight into how safe visitors to those parks feel.

cost-benefit (or benefit-cost): Any one of a number of approaches to comparing inputs to results; in other words, making the heavy lift necessary to see if taxpayer dollars are being spent in a way that translates into a reasonable value for the dollars spent.

dashboard: Often found online, and generally graphically presented, these are efforts to display data in such a way that it can be intuitively understood by users. In some instances, dashboards are simple displays of performance measures. In other cases, they permit users to dig through layers of underlying data.

data sharing: A multitude of governmental goals require the cooperation of agencies, departments, or programs. Their ability to have access to the same data accentuates collaborations, helps to avoid duplicative services, and benefits clients, who can be served more effectively. Dramatic insights can be achieved through analysis of shared data.

efficiency measures: These can help to communicate with the public a means for evaluating whether government services can be delivered at a lower cost or whether better services can be delivered without more investment.

evidence-based program and policymaking: The use of rigorously studied and evaluated programs and policies to inform decisions with objective information drawn from past practices. As the use of evidence expands, more attention is going to the need for caution in assuming that a program and methodology that worked well in one set of conditions will work equally well when tried in differing geographic, cultural, and demographic circumstances.

GIS (geographic information systems): With the capacity to manage spatial or geographic data, GIS systems can help managers see the relationship between different factors that may affect residents depending on where they live. GIS can inform funding and service decisions and lead to enhanced understanding of program performance. It also has multiple uses in real-time service delivery—for example, in deploying emergency response or mapping the needs of different communities when wildfires spread.

incentives: A means used to reward public sector employees, programs, or departments when performance-based information indicates that they have performed successfully or delivered on goals and objectives. The use of incentives requires caution, however, as they can induce negative behavior—for example, a desire to fudge data in order to reap a promised reward.

input: A performance measure that shows how much money and how many staff are dedicated to a particular program. These are vital measures for any kind of cost-benefit analysis, but by themselves tell nothing about the quality or even the quantity of the services delivered.

Lean: A popular approach, pioneered by Toyota, that attempts to cut waste in government and, by so doing, creates greater value to taxpayers without the need to raise their taxes. Lean training guides employees in structured problem-solving that eliminates unnecessary steps, improves processes, and adds value.

metrics: A cover-all word concerning any one of a number of measures that can be used to help improve effectiveness and efficiency of government.

open data: Information that can be easily accessed, shared, and used by any interested parties for any purpose. Open data portals in government can provide external users the ability to analyze, combine, and manipulate data, create their own digital applications, and potentially provide innovative solutions to government challenges.

outcomes: These measures show whether services deliver the benefits for which they were designed. (See also **results.**)

outputs: A performance measure that shows the level of work done, like permits approved, classes conducted, or books circulated in a library. They can be particularly helpful when it is difficult coming up with information about the benefits, or lack thereof, of programs. But they don't necessarily link to actual results.

performance audits: These independent examinations seek to answer questions about the efficiency and effectiveness of government programs or functions, with recommendations offered on how to address weaknesses and improve practices. Although there is a particular title, performance auditor, which is used in many governments, this effort is not restricted to their offices. It is highly important that performance audits are independent and cannot be unduly influenced by officials who disagree with audit topics or findings.

performance-based budgeting: The effort to use performance data as a base upon which to build a budget (see **performance-informed budgeting**).

performance-informed budgeting: A term preferred by many to "performance-based budgeting." It is a somewhat more realistic way of phrasing this approach, as "performance-based" appears to involve some kind of formula that converts performance into a ready-made budget. In fact, at best, executive and legislative branch budgeters are far more likely to use performance information to help guide their decisions, not to make them.

performance management: The topic of this book, this phrase covers a whole variety of approaches that involve using many different kinds of information (including numerical data, interviews, etc.) in order to help a city, county, state, or the federal government to deliver services as well and as economically as possible.

performance reports: These are documents—sometimes produced on a regular basis, sometimes sporadically—that can be employed by an agency to demonstrate that their funds are being used appropriately and are culminating in desired results.

practitioners: Notwithstanding the medical use of this term, these are the men and women, primarily working for the executive branch, who labor to provide goods and services to the public. Practitioners are to be differentiated from elected officials who are primarily decision-makers, not implementers of those decisions.

process improvement: Differing from instances in which processes improve simply through trial, error, and evolution, process improvement implies a purposeful effort to accomplish the same thing.

response times: One of the most common performance measures used to evaluate the work of public employees. It is often used to gauge the performance of first responders, like police and fire, to see how long it takes them to get from a phone call requesting help to the delivery of that help. But it can also be a good measure of the efficiency with which other services are delivered, for example, the time required to get someone a driver's license at a department of motor vehicles. There is a hazard in relying exclusively on response times without taking quality into consideration, as speed does not always equate to quality of service.

results: Sometimes used interchangeably with "outcomes," these are the best measure of the success of a program in achieving its goals or objectives.

Stat: Popularized by New York City's CompStat, the Stat approach generally brings the team responsible for a particular effort together with leaders to analyze program data and move forward with actions that lead to program improvement. Although popular, Stat programs can be risky, as they can push alarmed employees into gaming the data they bring to the table.

strategic plans: These are constructed in a wide variety of ways, but their goal is to chart out how an entity intends to move forward, usually in the near-term future. Sometimes, strategic plans are tied directly to performance measures in order to track the progress made toward achieving the strategic goals set forth in the plan. Strategic plans may be formed for an entire entity, or for a single department.

sustainability: Generally used in the context of fiscal affairs, within the realm of performance management it refers to the idea that a performance reform initiative will last from administration to administration, which is not an easy task.

targets: It can be useful in managing performance to have a clear idea of what a program is expected to accomplish given its resources. On an annual or biannual basis, targets can motivate programs to strive toward achieving a preset level of success. But too much emphasis on the percentage of targets achieved can cause potential problems—for example, lowballing of targets so they can be easily reached.

validation: The mere existence of a piece of data used to help make governmental decisions is a good first step. But, all too often inaccurate data finds its way into the mix. The concept of validation covers any one of a variety of ways to ensure accuracy both in the final data and the methodology used to derive it.

Notes

■ ■ ■

CHAPTER 2: CHALLENGES

[1] Virginia Department of Planning and Budget, State Agency Planning & Performance Measures, http://dpb.virginia.gov/sp/sp.cfm.

[2] "Percentage of Foster Care Children Who Are Placed with Families," Department of Social Services Strategic Agency Planning & Performance Measures, http://publicreports.dpb.virginia.gov/rdPage.aspx?rdReport=vp_OneMeasure&MeasureID=76546901.001.002&ReportName=Strategic%20Planning%20Measure%20Details&ReportNumber=VP1.31.

[3] "Number of Jobs Created by New and Existing Companies," Virginia Economic Development Partnership, Strategic Agency Planning & Performance Measures, http://publicreports.dpb.virginia.gov/rdPage.aspx?rdReport=vp_OneMeasure&MeasureID=31053412.002.001&ReportName=Strategic%20Planning%20Measure%20Details&ReportNumber=VP1.31.

[4] Strategic planning measure details, 7, http://publicreports.dpb.virginia.gov/rdPage.aspx?rdReport=vp_MeasureDetails132&ShowInput=DontShow&ShowToggle=Show&Submitted=Show&ShowHelp=Show&selAgency=All.

[5] Katherine Barrett and Richard Greene, "How to Turn Government Data into Clickbait," *Governing*, October 2018, www.governing.com/columns/smart-mgmt/gov-management-dashboard.html.

[6] According to Equipt to Innovate, high-performing governments are: dynamically planned, broadly partnered, resident-involved, race-informed, smartly resourced, employee-engaged, and data-driven. Note: We were among the five judges for the 2019 survey and also wrote a column based on Equipt research for *Governing*.

[7] Equipt to Innovate, *2019 Profiles in High Performing Government: Cities on the Move*, *Governing* in partnership with Living Cities, 2019, 7, www.governing.com/papers/2019-Profiles-in-High-Performance-Government-Cities-on-the-move-116842.html.

[8] Pew Charitable Trusts, *The Role of Outcome Monitoring in Evidence-Based Policymaking: How States Can Use Performance Management Systems to Achieve Results*, issue brief from the Pew-MacArthur Results First Initiative, August 2018, 1–2, www.pewtrusts.org/-/media/assets/2018/08/rf_outcome_monitoring-brief_v4.pdf.

9 Katherine Barrett and Richard Greene, "The State of the States," *Financial World*, May 11, 1993, 55 (no link available).
10 ICMA is now the full name of the organization. It originated as the "International City Managers' Association."
11 National Performance Management Advisory Committee, *A Performance Management Framework for State and Local Government: From Measurement and Reporting to Management and Improving*, www.gfoa.org/sites/default/files/APerformanceManagementFramework.pdf.
12 Frank Konkel, "The Totally Awesome Future of GIS," FCWINSIDER, Feb. 27, 2013, https://fcw.com/Blogs/FCW-Insider/2013/02/future-of-GIS.aspx.
13 Results Washington, Outcome Measures, https://results.wa.gov/outcome-measures.
14 Stephen Goldsmith, "Data and the Human Side of Criminal Justice," *Governing*, February 20, 2019, www.governing.com/blogs/bfc/col-long-beach-justice-lab-human-centered-design.html.
15 J. B. Wogan, "How-to Guide on Using Evidence in City Policymaking," A Mathematica *On the Evidence* Podcast, March 13, 2019, www.mathematica-mpr.com/commentary/how-to-guide-on-using-evidence-in-city-policymaking?MPRSource=TCSide.
16 Katherine Barrett and Richard Greene, Government's Data Drive Frenemies, *Governing*, March 17, 2016, www.governing.com/columns/smart-mgmt/gov-performance-measurement-program-evaluator.html.

CHAPTER 3: BENEFITS

1 CountyStat, Performance Management and Data Analytics, https://stat.montgomerycountymd.gov/.
2 Montgomery County. Pedestrian Safety Initiative Update, May 8, 2013, 14, https://reports.data.montgomerycountymd.gov/en/dataset/Ped-Safety-05-08-13-1-/suu5-xh56.
3 Vision Zero is an initiative that started in Sweden and has sparked strategies and actions in many U.S. and other governments to reduce and eventually eliminate traffic fatalities.
4 Vision Zero. Montgomery County Vision Zero Data Explorer, https://countystat.maps.arcgis.com/apps/MapJournal/index.html?appid=a5601587930a42c6b5b1ad87ba58a6c5.
5 San Jose City Auditor, City of San Jose Annual Report on City Services 2017–2018, December 2018, www.sanjoseca.gov/DocumentCenter/View/81795.
6 San Jose city services report, 6, 19.
7 Pew-MacArthur Results First Initiative, The Role of Outcome Monitoring in Evidence-Based Policymaking, August 2018, 9, www.pewtrusts.org/-/media/assets/2018/08/rf_outcome_monitoring-brief_v4.pdf.
8 Minnesota Department of Education, *Homework Starts with Home*, https://education.mn.gov/MDE/fam/home/.
9 Katherine Barrett and Richard Greene, "Are Your Schools Tracking Absenteeism the Right Way?" November 2017, www.governing.com/columns/smart-mgmt/gov-students-awol-absentee-rates.html.
10 Maria Cancian, Steven T. Cook, Mai Seki, Lynn Wimer, "Making Parents Pay: The Unintended Consequences of Charging Parents for Foster Care," Children and Youth Services Review, October 13, 2016, https://reader.elsevier.com/reader/sd/pii/S0190740916303425?token=7D68432CC9A8D7893448696720961215CC592DA24A9322A8F2316F9DB87498486FB5210193D548DD36BAB66CC1B45A13.
11 Pew Charitable Trusts, How States Use Data to Inform Decisions, February 2018, 9, www.pewtrusts.org/-/media/assets/2018/02/dasa_how_states_use_data_report_v5.pdf.

12 Indiana Management and Performance Hub. Annual Report, 2018, 4, www.in.gov/mph/files/MPH-2018-Annual-Report.pdf.

13 J. B. Wogan, "Forget Technology; Denver Turns to Its Employees to Fix Problems," *Governing*, February 2014, www.governing.com/topics/mgmt/gov-denver-seeks-employee-help.html.

14 Denver Mayor's Office, "Mayor Hancock Celebrates Five Years of Initiative That Has Saved Denver Taxpayers $22.5 million." www.denvergov.org/content/denvergov/en/mayors-office/newsroom/2017/mayor-hancock-celebrates-five-years-of-initiative-that-has-saved.html.

15 King County, *Equity and Social Justice Strategic Plan, 2016–2022*, https://aqua.kingcounty.gov/dnrp/library/dnrp-directors-office/equity-social-justice/201609-ESJ-SP-FULL.pdf.

16 Lean is an entire performance management system that was developed in the private sector. Most governments that talk about using Lean have adapted tools from the Lean philosophy. See the glossary.

17 Richard Greene, coauthor of this book, is currently chair of the Center for Accountability and Performance.

18 United States Census Bureau, Stats in Action: New Orleans, LA: Smoke Alarm Outreach Program, September 2016. https://www.census.gov/library/video/2016/sia-nola-saop.html. (Note: This website also includes a short video.)

CHAPTER 4: HISTORY

1 The Training School for Public Service was later moved from New York City to Syracuse and became the Maxwell School of Citizenship and Public Affairs.

2 Sports fans note that his uncle, of the same name, inspired James Naismith to invent the game of basketball in 1891.

3 Barrett and Greene, Inc., What's New Is Old, https://greenebarrett.com/budget-transparency/.

4 Robert J. O'Neill Jr., "Performance Management in Government: The Old Is New Again," *Governing*, September 8, 2014, www.governing.com/columns/smart-mgmt/col-performance-management-government-history-stat-data-analysis-visualization.html.

5 Philip Joyce, "Performance Budgeting in the United States: Current Federal and State Experiences," prepared for the annual conference of the Association for Public Policy Analysis and Management," November 10, 2018.

6 Minnesota House of Representatives Research Department. Performance-Based Budgeting, information brief, January 2016, www.leg.state.mn.us/docs/2016/other/160130.pdf.

7 Alabama Department of Finance, Executive Budget Office. Budget Management Act, Sections 41-19-1 through 41-19-12, https://budget.alabama.gov/budget_management_act/.

8 Until the early 2000s, GAO was the acronym for the General Accounting Office, which had been established as the federal government's auditing body in 1921. In 2004, the name was changed to Government Accountability Office. The acronym remained the same.

9 Elaine Yi Lu and Katherine Willoughby. *Public Performance Budgeting: Principles and Practice*. Routledge, 2019.

10 Lu and Willoughby, 28.

11 United States General Accounting Office. Quality Management: Survey of Federal Organizations. October 1992, www.gao.gov/assets/80/78554.pdf.

12 Between 1990 and 1995, we led management evaluation exercises at *Financial World* using multiple interviews with experts to guide the process, but with no academic involvement. We evaluated states four times, cities three times, and federal government

agencies twice, before *Financial World* went out of business. Then in 1996, the Pew Charitable Trusts began exploring funding a new and similar effort along with us, *Governing* magazine, *Government Executive* magazine, and the Maxwell School of Citizenship and Public Policy. Our state and local portion of the Government Performance Project was piloted in 1997 and work started in 1998 on a first evaluation of states. Later, the academic part of the project was shifted from the Maxwell School to a virtual faculty including Philip Joyce, Michael Pagano, Katherine Willoughby, and Sally Selden, and headed by Don Kettl.

[13] Katherine Barrett and Richard Greene, "State of the States 1995: Tick, Tick, Tick," *Financial World* magazine, September 26, 1995, 40, 44.

[14] Katherine Barrett and Richard Greene, "Measuring Performance: The State Management Report Card for 2008," *Governing*, March 2008, 58, www.pewtrusts.org/-/media/legacy/uploadedfiles/pcs_assets/2008/gradingthestates2008pdf.pdf.

[15] Association of Local Government Auditors, The History: Dream, Journey, Pathway, 1985–2001, https://algaonline.org/DocumentCenter/View/6012.

[16] Katherine Barrett & Richard Greene, "Grading the States: The Mandate to Measure," *Governing*, March 2008, 27, www.pewtrusts.org/-/media/legacy/uploadedfiles/wwwpewtrustsorg/reports/government_performance/gradingthestates2008pdf.pdf.

[17] Cynthia Firey Eakin, "Zero-Based Budgeting: Everything Old Is New Again," The Conversation, November 23, 2015, http://theconversation.com/zero-based-budgeting-everything-old-is-new-again-50633.

[18] The Pew-MacArthur initiative is partially based on work pioneered by the Washington Institute for Public Policy, a nonpartisan public research group that was created by the legislature in 1983 and has developed a system for analyzing the costs and benefits of a wide variety of programs.

[19] Governmental Accounting Standards Board, Suggested Guidelines for Voluntary Reporting of Performance Information, June 2010, www.gasb.org/cs/ContentServer?c=GASBContent_C&cid=1176157102416&d=&pagename=GASB%2FGASBContent_C%2FGASBNewsPage.

[20] Government Finance Officers Association, *Service Efforts and Accomplishments Reporting*, Public Policy Statements-Accounting, Auditing and Financial Reporting, June 23, 1993, www.gfoa.org/public-policy-statements-accounting-auditing-and-financial-reporting#SEA.

[21] GFOA, *Performance Measurement and the Governmental Accounting Standards Board*, Public Policy Statements—Accounting, Auditing and Financial Reporting, June 18, 2002, www.gfoa.org/public-policy-statements-accounting-auditing-and-financial-reporting#PerformanceMeasurement.

[22] Governmental Accounting Standards Board, *Reporting Performance Information: Suggested Criteria for Effective Communication*, Special Report Summary, October 2003, www.seagov.org/sea_gasb_project/criteria_summary.pdf.

CHAPTER 5: OUTCOMES

[1] Ken Miller's books are *We Don't Make Widgets*, Governing Management Series, 2010, and *Extreme Government Makeover: Increasing Our Capacity to Do More Good*, Governing Management Series, 2011.

[2] Mel Carnahan was governor of Missouri from 1993 until his death in a plane crash in 2000. In the 1999 "Grading the States" issue of *Governing*, Missouri was one of the top states in the Managing for Results category, praised for strategic planning, interagency teams, objective measures, and "show me" goals.

[3] Center on Budget and Policy Priorities, *Temporary Assistance for Needy Families*, Policy Basics, updated August 15, 2018, 5, www.cbpp.org/sites/default/files/atoms/files/7-22-10tanf2.pdf.

4 City of Syracuse Performance Dashboard, http://dashboards.syrgov.net/.

5 The National Center for Public Performance previously operated out of Rutgers University in Newark, New Jersey, from 1989 to 2017; Marc Holzer, who has been executive director of this effort since 1974 when he founded the center at City University of New York, relocated to Boston in 2017 and brought the National Center with him to its new home at Suffolk University.

6 U.S. Department of Health and Human Services, "HHS Announces the Nation's New Health Promotion and Disease Prevention Agenda," December 2, 2010, www.healthypeople.gov/sites/default/files/DefaultPressRelease_1.pdf.

7 Office of Disease Prevention and Health Promotion, Healthy People.gov, www.healthypeople.gov/.

8 Results Washington, https://results.wa.gov/.

9 Jane Wiseman, "Case Study: Performance Management and Lean Process Improvement—Results Washington: An Operational Excellence in Government Success Story," Ash Center for Democratic Governance and Innovation, Harvard Kennedy School, 16–17, www.innovations.harvard.edu/sites/default/files/Case-Study-Results-Washington-Performance-Management-Lean.pdf.

10 State of Washington Office of the Governor, *Building Safe and Strong Communities through Successful Reentry*, Executive Order 16-05, April 26, 2016, www.governor.wa.gov/sites/default/files/exe_order/eo_16-05.pdf.

11 Results Washington, Supporting Successful Reentry, https://results.wa.gov/outcome-measures/supporting-successful-reentry.

CHAPTER 6: PERFORMANCE BUDGETING

1 National Association of State Budget Officers, *Investing in Results: Using Performance Data to Inform State Budgeting*, Spring 2014, https://community.nasbo.org/pressclips/reports-data/investing-in-results.

2 Elaine Yi Lu and Katherine Willoughby, *Public Performance Budgeting: Principles and Practice*, Taylor & Francis, 2019, 9.

3 Lu and Willoughby, *Public Performance Budgeting*, 27.

4 Paul Kiel and Jesse Eisinger, "How the IRS Was Gutted," ProPublica, December 11, 2018, www.propublica.org/article/how-the-irs-was-gutted.

5 Yilin Hou, Robin S. Lunsford, Katy C. Sides, and Kelsey A. Jones, "State Performance-Based Budgeting in Boom and Bust Years: An Analytical Framework and Survey of the States," *Public Administration Review*, May 9, 2011, https://onlinelibrary.wiley.com/doi/abs/10.1111/j.1540-6210.2011.02357.x.

6 Philip Joyce, "Performance Budgeting in the United States: Current Federal and State Experiences," prepared for the annual conference of the Association for Public Policy Analysis and Management, November 10, 2018, 4.

7 Katherine Barrett and Richard Greene, "Grading the States: A Management Report Card," *Governing*, February 1999, 68.

8 Katherine Barrett and Richard Greene, "States Start Making Colleges Work for Funding," *Governing*, April 2016, www.governing.com/columns/smart-mgmt/gov-college-performance-based-funding.html.

9 New Mexico Legislative Finance Committee Program Evaluation Unit, Program Evaluation: Review of the Higher Education Funding Formula, August 22, 2018, www.nmlegis.gov/Entity/LFC/Documents/Program_Evaluation_Reports/Review%20of%20the%20Higher%20Education%20Funding%20Formula%20-%20August%202018.pdf.

10 National Association of State Budget Officers. *Statewide Initiatives to Advance the Use of Data & Evidence for Decision-Making: A Working Inventory*, last updated November 2018, www.nasbo.org/reports-data/using-data-and-evidence.

11 NASBO, *Using Data and Evidence in Governors' Fiscal 2020 Budgets*, April 10, 2019, 2, https://higherlogicdownload.s3.amazonaws.com/NASBO/9d2d2db1-c943-4f1b-b750-0fca152d64c2/UploadedImages/Issue%20Briefs%20/Governors__Budgets_for_FY_2020_-Using_Data_and_Evidence.pdf.

12 FY 2018–2019 Budget Request, Governor John Hickenlooper, November 1, 2017, 9, https://drive.google.com/file/d/0B0TNL0CtD9wXbkNUb0NIQmVrVXM/view.

13 Kathryn White, "The Use of Data and Evidence in Governors' Fiscal 2019 Budgets," Budget Blog, NASBO, April 8, 2018, http://budgetblog.nasbo.org/budgetblogs/blogs/kathryn-white/2018/04/09/the-use-of-data-and-evidence-in-governors-fiscal-2?CommunityKey=eca4d2c7-296d-4ab5-aeab-2024a4e7b0b8&tab=.

14 Pew Charitable Trusts, The Role of Outcome Monitoring in Evidence-Based Policymaking: An Issue Brief from the Pew-MacArthur Results First initiative, August 2018, 5, www.pewtrusts.org/-/media/assets/2018/08/rf_outcome_monitoring-brief_v4.pdf.

15 NASBO, Budget Processes in the States, Chapter 5, Monitoring the Budget, Spring 2015, 117–126, https://higherlogicdownload.s3.amazonaws.com/NASBO/9d2d2db1-c943-4f1b-b750-0fca152d64c2/UploadedImages/Budget%20Processess/2015_Budget_Processes_-_S.pdf.

16 Budget Processes, 117.

17 Budget Processes, Table 25: Additional Details and Notes, 124–26.

18 At the time of the 2016 Beasley-Moynihan study, Moynihan was professor of public affairs at the LaFollette School of Public Affairs at the University of Wisconsin, Madison.

19 Ivor Beasley and Don Moynihan, "Toward Next Generation Performance Budgeting," Public Financial Management Blog, International Monetary Fund, January 24, 2017, https://blog-pfm.imf.org/pfmblog/2017/01/toward-next-generation-performance-budgeting.html.

20 Austin Strategic Direction 2023, https://austinstrategicplan.bloomfire.com/posts/3301043-austin-strategic-direction-2023-final.

21 Austin Finance Online. *FY2018–19 Approved Budget*, www.austintexas.gov/financeonline/afo_content.cfm?s=1&p=165.

22 Appendix to Strategic Direction 2023, austinstrategicplan.bloomfire.com/series/3304505-appendix-to-strategic-direction-2023.

23 State of Illinois Governor Pat Quinn, Budgeting for Results Commission Report, November 2011, 3, www2.illinois.gov/sites/budget/Documents/Budgeting%20for%20Results/Related%20Documents/Budgeting%20for%20Results%20Commission%20Report%20Nov%202011.pdf.

24 Budgeting for Results Commission. 8th Annual Commission Report, November 1, 2018, www2.illinois.gov/sites/budget/Documents/Budgeting%20for%20Results/2018%20BFR%20Annual%20Commission%20Report%2011.1.18.pdf.

CHAPTER 7: PITFALLS

1 Michael Jacobson, "Sustaining the Change Agent," MRSC Insight Blog, August 14, 2017, http://mrsc.org/Home/Stay-Informed/MRSC-Insight/August-2017/Sustaining-the-Change-Agent.aspx.

2 Katherine Barrett and Richard Greene, "Mapping Technology Expands Its Policy Reach," *Governing*, January 2019, www.governing.com/columns/smart-mgmt/gov-gis-mapping.html.

3 Beth Blauer was formerly executive director at the Center for Government Excellence (GovEx) at Johns Hopkins University. In her new position as executive director of the Centers for Civic Impact, she oversees GovEx, the GovEx Academy, and the Center for Applied Public Research, all at Johns Hopkins.

4 Hanna Azemati, "How Social Services and Performance Contracting Fit Together," *Governing*, October 25, 2018, www.governing.com/blogs/bfc/col-performance-based-contracting-social-services-outcomes.html.

5 J.B. Wogan, "How Stat Got Stuck—in the Place That Made It Famous," *Governing*, April 2017, https://www.governing.com/topics/mgmt/gov-baltimore-citistat-statestat-maryland.html.

6 National Conference of State Legislatures, Legislative Performance Budgeting, September 2008, http://www.ncsl.org/research/fiscal-policy/legislative-performance-budgeting.aspx.

7 Philip Joyce, "Performance Budgeting in the United States: Current Federal and State Experiences," prepared for the Annual Conference of the Association for Public Policy Analysis and Management, November 10, 2018.

CHAPTER 8: BUY-IN

1 CPS HR Consulting and ASQ Government Division, Achievements and Barriers: The Results of Lean and Quality Initiatives in Government, March 17, 2017, iii, www.cpshr.us/services/resources/org-strat/OrgAssessment/LEAN_March2017.pdf.

2 CPS HR and ASQ study, iv–v.

3 Steve Kelman, "Steve's peeve about a common contracting phrase," FCW, October 2, 2018, https://fcw.com/blogs/lectern/2018/10/kelman-the-l-word.aspx.

4 Melissa Wavelet, "A Practitioner's Framework for Measuring Results: Using C-Stat at the Colorado Department of Human Services," The IBM Center for the Business of Government, 2019, http://www.businessofgovernment.org/report/practitioner%E2%80%99s-framework-measuring-results-using-%E2%80%9Cc-stat%E2%80%9D-colorado-department-human-services.

5 Chris Smith, "The Controversial Crime Fighting Program That Changed Big City Policing Forever," *New York Magazine*, March 2018, http://nymag.com/intelligencer/2018/03/the-crime-fighting-program-that-changed-new-york-forever.html.

6 Bicha, personal conversation, August 23, 2018.

CHAPTER 9: VALIDATION

1 Pew Charitable Trusts, *How States Use Data to Inform Decisions: A National Review of the Use of Administrative Data to Improve State Decision-Making*, February 2018, 2, www.pewtrusts.org/-/media/assets/2018/02/dasa_how_states_use_data_report_v5.pdf.

2 California State Auditor, *California's Foster Care System: The State and Counties Have Failed to Adequately Oversee the Prescription of Psychotropic Medications to Children in Foster Care*, August 2016, iii, www.auditor.ca.gov/pdfs/reports/2015–131.pdf.

3 Kansas Legislative Division of Post Audit, *Foster Care and Adoption in Kansas: Reviewing Various Issues Related to the State's Foster Care and Adoption System, Part 3*, A report to the Legislative Post-Audit Committee, April 2017, www.kslpa.org/assets/files/reports/r-17-006.pdf.

4 Oregon Secretary of State, Audits Division, *Foster Care in Oregon: Chronic management failures and high caseloads jeopardize the safety of some of the state's most vulnerable children*, January 2018, 10 (also see audit highlights) https://sos.oregon.gov/audits/Documents/2018-05.pdf.

5 Christopher J. Ruhm, "Geographic Variation in Opioid and Heroin Involved Drug-Poisoning Mortality Rates," *American Journal of Preventive Medicine*, Volume 53, Issue 6, December 2017, 745–53, www.ajpmonline.org/article/S0749-3797(17)30313–6/fulltext.

6 Puja Seth, Rose A. Rudd, Rita K. Noonan, and Tamara M. Haegerich, "Quantifying the Epidemic of Prescription Opioid Overdose Deaths," *American Journal of Public Health*, April 1, 2018, 500–02,https://ajph.aphapublications.org/doi/10.2105/ AJPH.2017.304265.

7 Katherine Barrett and Richard Greene, "Data-Based Decision Making Works Great, Til Somebody Cheats," *Governing*, August 2018, www.governing.com/columns/smart-mgmt/gov-performance-based-management.html.

8 Parishes in Louisiana are the equivalent of counties in other states.

9 Portland City Auditor, Ombudsman Report: 911 Hold Times Longer Than Reported, June 27, 5, www.portlandoregon.gov/ombudsman/article/642095.

10 "A Timeline of How the Atlanta School Cheating Scandal Unfolded," *Atlanta Journal-Constitution*, April 2, 2015, www.ajc.com/news/timeline-how-the-atlanta-school-cheating-scandal-unfolded/jn4vTk7GZUQoQRJTVR7UHK/.

11 Phillip Joyce, "When Performance Measurement Goes Wrong in Government," *Governing*, July 16, 2014, www.governing.com/columns/smart-mgmt/col-performance-measurement-scandals-lessons.html.

12 Robert Prentice, "Gaming the System: The VA Scandal," Ethics Unwrapped, The McCombs School of Business, https://ethicsunwrapped.utexas.edu/case-study/ gaming-system-va-scandal.

13 Joyce, *Governing*, July 16, 2014.

14 Katherine Barrett and Richard Greene, "The Causes, Costs and Consequences of Bad Government Data," *Governing*, June 24, 2015, www.governing.com/topics/mgmt/gov-bad-data.html.

15 California State Auditor, Data-Reliability: State Agencies Computer-Generated Data Varied in their Completeness and Accuracy, Report Number: 2016–401, September 27, 2016, www.auditor.ca.gov/reports/2016–401/index.html.

16 Texas State Auditor's Office, Performance Measures at the Commission on Fire Protection, September 2018, i, www.sao.texas.gov/Reports/Main/19-002.pdf.

17 Barrett and Greene, "Causes, Costs and Consequences," *Governing*, 2015.

18 US Government Accountability Offic,. Data Act: OMB, Treasury and Agencies Need to Improve Completeness and Accuracy of Spending Data and Data Limitations." November 2017, www.gao.gov/assets/690/688217.pdf.

19 Greg B. Smith, "City Lying about Safety at Shelters by Undercounting 'Critical Incidents'; Homeless Services Cops Say Crime Getting Worse," *New York Daily News*, April 25, 2018, www.nydailynews.com/new-york/city-lying-safety-homeless-shelters-article-1.3952889.

CHAPTER 10: DATA PROGRESS

1 Katherine Barrett and Richard Greene, "Mapping Technology Expands Its Policy Reach," *Governing*, January 2019, www.governing.com/columns/smart-mgmt/gov-gis-mapping.html

2 The Pew Charitable Trusts, How States Use Data To Inform Decisions: A National Review of the Use of Data to Inform Decision Making. February 2018, 2, www. pewtrusts.org/-/media/assets/2018/02/dasa_how_states_use_data_report_v5.pdf.

3 City of New York, Vision Zero, https://www1.nyc.gov/site/visionzero/index.page.

4 Jenni Bergal, "Troopers Use Big Data to Predict Crashes," Stateline, The Pew Charitable Trusts, February 9, 2017, www.pewtrusts.org/en/research-and-analysis/blogs/ stateline/2017/02/09/troopers-use-big-data-to-predict-crash-sites.

5 We were judges for the Equipt to Innovate survey in 2019 and also wrote a number of "Equipt to Innovate" columns for *Governing*.

[6] Equipt to Innovate, 2019 Profiles in High Performance Government: Cities on the Move, *Governing* in partnership with Living Cities, 2019, www.governing.com/papers/2019-Profiles-in-High-Performance-Government-Cities-on-the-move-116842.html.

[7] Agencies mentioned in Gov. Kate Brown's March 2018 executive order were the Oregon Health Authority, the Oregon Health Policy Board, the Department of Human Services, the Department of Corrections, the Oregon Youth Authority, the Youth Development Council, the Department of Housing and Community Services, the Department of Consumer and Business Services, and the Department of Education.

[8] Kathryn White, "The Use of Data and Evidence in Governors' Fiscal 2019 Budgets," Budget Blog, NASBO, April 8, 2018, http://budgetblog.nasbo.org/budgetblogs/blogs/kathryn-white/2018/04/09/the-use-of-data-and-evidence-in-governors-fiscal-2?CommunityKey=eca4d2c7-296d-4ab5-aeab-2024a4e7b0b8&tab=.

[9] Equipt to Innovate, 2019, 19,

[10] Equipt to Innovate, 2018 Profiles in High Performance Government: Cities on the Move. Published by *Governing* in partnership with Living Cities, 2018, 32, www.governing.com/papers/Profiles-in-High-Performance-Government-Cities-on-the-move-100801.html.

[11] Katherine Barrett and Richard Greene, "Where's the Data? What the Government Isn't Tracking," *Governing*, March 2009, www.governing.com/columns/smart-mgmt/gov-missing-government-data.html.

CHAPTER 11: EVALUATION

[1] American Evaluation Association, AEA Competencies, www.eval.org/page/competencies.

[2] Idaho Office of Performance Evaluations, Child Welfare Systems: Reducing the Risk of Adverse Outcomes, March 2018, https://legislature.idaho.gov/ope/reports/r1803/.

[3] Results for America. *2018 Invest in What Works State Standard of Excellence*, July 2018, https://results4america.org/tools/state-standard-of-excellence-2018-invest-in-what-works-state-standard-of-excellence/.

[4] State Standard of Excellence, 9, 5–6.

[5] Pew Charitable Trusts/MacArthur Foundation Results First Initiative, How States Engage in Evidence-Based Policymaking, January 2017, 1, www.pewtrusts.org/-/media/assets/2017/01/how_states_engage_in_evidence_based_policymaking.pdf.

[6] Pew Charitable Trusts/MacArthur Foundation, *Evidence-Based Policymaking: A Guide for Effective Government*, November 2014, 17, www.pewtrusts.org/-/media/assets/2014/11/evidencebasedpolicymakingaguideforeffectivegovernment.pdf.

[7] Jonathan McCay, Rayna Jefferson, Hayley Ballinger, Ruby Nolasco, and Heather Lower, "Learn, Innovate, Improve: Lessons from Adam County's Efforts to Increase Engagement in the Colorado Works Program," June 2018, www.mathematica-mpr.com/our-publications-and-findings/publications/lessons-from-adams-countys-efforts-to-increase-engagement-in-the-colorado-works-program.

[8] Pew Charitable Trusts, Behavioral Analytics Help Save Unemployment Insurance Funds, October 26, 2016, www.pewtrusts.org/en/research-and-analysis/issue-briefs/2016/10/behavioral-analytics-help-save-unemployment-insurance-funds.

Index

■ ■ ■

Drucker, Peter, 25
drug overdose deaths, validation
of data and, 100–101
Duke University, *82*

Eagleton Institute of Politics
(Rutgers University), 26–27
Edelstein, Sam, 46–47
Eenoo, Ed Van, 67
efficiency, 46–47, 143
Equipt to Innovate (survey), 4,
117–18, 121
Erickson, Sharon, 12, 41, *122*
Escobar, Gipsy, 100
Estonia, performance
budgeting in, 64–65
evaluation in performance-
informed management,
126–37
attention to, 127–31
cost-benefit approach, *134*
evidence-based policymaking
and, *132–33*
on frontlines, 128–31
funding and, 127–31
human-centered nature of PIM
and, *135*
overview, 126–27
Randomized Control Trials
(RCTs) and, 130
evidence-based policymaking,
132–33, 143
Evidence-Based Policymaking Act
of 2018, *132*
Evidence-Based Policymaking
Commission Act of 2016, *30*
excessive hype, 76–77
external funding, 34–35

federal government. *See specific
entity or topic*
federal level, progress at, 29–30, *30*
Fercak, Alexandra, 77

Financial World (magazine),
1, 28, 41
Florida
Department of Juvenile
Justice, 62
performance budgeting in, 62
performance measurement in, 44
Floyd, Gregory, *111*
Foundations of Evidence-Based
Policymaking Act of 2018, *30*
Fountain, Jay, 28, 77
France, performance budgeting
in, 64–65
Frans, Myron, 13, 15
Funkhouser, Mark, 27, 36, 37

Gaebler, Ted, 29
Gelb, Adam, 122
Geographic Information Systems
(GIS), 72, 113, *125,* 143
George, Tim, 17
Giuliani, Rudolph, 89
Global Positioning System (GPS),
113–14
glossary, 142–46
goals, 43–44, 46
Goldsmith, Stephen, 7
Gore, Al, 29
Gottesman, David, 11
Governing (magazine), xx, 1, 4,
28, 61, 74, *106,* 116, 141
Government Accountability Office
(GAO), 27–28, *30,* 108–9, *110*
Governmental Accounting
Standards Board (GASB),
28–29, 37–39, 77
Government Executive
(magazine), 28
Government Finance
Officers Association (GFOA),
37–39
Government Finance Review
(magazine), 27